Praise for *The New Imperialists*

The New Imperialists is a remarkably important outline of the scale of the challenge facing America. Pirchner and Berman have drawn on their lifetime of work in national security to outline the emerging alliance of anti-democratic autocrats determined to work together to shrink America's role in the world and to make the world safe for dictatorships. There are details in this book which will be eye opening even for those of us who have been working on national security for a long time.

The Honorable Newt Gingrich,
former Speaker of the U.S. House of Representatives

Much has been written about the threats to the U.S. posed by Russia, China and Iran. Pirchner and Berman make a unique contribution by connecting the dots among the three, and by offering an invaluable perspective on their long history as imperial powers. They are equally compelling in their recommendations on how the U.S. can counter these threats, from strengthening our alliances to enhancing our own military and informational capabilities to better confront these three imperial adversaries.

The Honorable Ryan C. Crocker,
former U.S. Ambassador to Afghanistan, Iraq, Pakistan, Syria, Kuwait, and Lebanon. Board Chair, Middle East Broadcasting Networks

Pirchner and Berman are laying out a pivotal historical question: After centuries of citizen-based democracies becoming stronger and building peaceful alliances with each other, are authoritarians with visions of ruling over others making a comeback? The answer is "yes" – but it is not game over. By documenting how the imperialists are gaining ground, they also point the way forward. The citizen-based West can meet and defeat the challenge, but first we must understand it."

The Honorable Kurt Volker,
former U.S. Ambassador to NATO and former
U.S. Representative for Ukraine Negotiations

In *The New Imperialists*, Pirchner and Berman expertly diagnose and then proscribe solutions to deal with the preeminent foreign policy challenge of the 21st Century – the rise of totalitarian, expansionist dictatorships working together to threaten our security, prosperity and freedom. Western societies must mobilize society-wide efforts to counter them. The free world has the capability to rise to the occasion. But does it have the will? *The New Imperialists* is an indispensable call to action.

Josh Rogin,
Lead Global Security Analyst, WP Intelligence, Author,
Chaos Under Heaven: Trump, Xi, and the Battle for the
21st Century (Mariner Books, 2021)

The New Imperialists

ISBN (paperback): 978-1-968919-21-4
ISBN (Ebook): 978-1-968919-24-5

AMERICAN FOREIGN POLICY COUNCIL

AFPC Press
American Foreign Policy Council
509 C Street NE
Washington, DC 20002

Published by Armin Lear Press, Inc.
215 W Riverside Drive, #4362
Estes Park, CO 80517

The New Imperialists

How China, Russia and Iran
are trying to remake the world

Herman Pirchner, Jr. and Ilan Berman

AFPC

Contents

A New Imperial Moment   1

China: The Middle Kingdom on the March   7

Russia: Renewed dreams of Eurasian empire   23

Iran: An Islamist Impulse for Expansion   43

The Fellow Travelers: North Korea and Venezuela   63

Modes of Cooperation   81

Confronting The New Imperialists   95

About the Authors   113

Author's Note

In fully grasping the historical narratives that follow, the reader will be greatly aided by the accompanying collection of maps available at:

https://www.afpc.org/publications/special-reports/
the-new-imperialists-map-collection

A New Imperial Moment

Today, the liberal world order established after the Second World War finds itself challenged like never before. Despite the rapid proliferation of new technologies such as artificial intelligence, the ubiquity of automated and increasingly deadly means of warfighting, and a wholesale transformation of the international media environment, the threat facing the Western world is, at bottom, not new. Rather, the force now seeking to undermine the existing global order is a decidedly old one that has been given new life and impetus by current circumstances.

That force is **imperial revivalism**, and it can be seen today in the rekindled aspirations of China, Russia and Iran to expand their respective territories, aggregate additional subjects to their burgeoning empires of influence and control, and to reshape the broader international "rules of the road" to their authoritarian whims. And while other nations (like the Venezuela of leftist strongman Nicolas Maduro and North Korea under the brutal Kim dynasty) likewise harbor at least some imperial aspirations of their own, it is the combined – and increasingly collaborative – quest for renewed imperial greatness on the part of Beijing, Moscow and Tehran that represents the most pressing danger to the contemporary global order.

It is also arguably the greatest threat confronting the United States in the years ahead. How Washington chooses to address, respond to and counter the imperial designs of what some have called the new "axis of upheaval"[1] will help determine a great deal about the complexion of the

---

1   Andrea Kendall-Taylor and Richard Fontaine, "Axis of Upheaval: How America's Adversaries Are Uniting to Overturn the Global Order," *Foreign Affairs*, May/June 2024, https://www.foreignaffairs.com/china/axis-upheaval-russia-iran-north-korea-taylor-fontaine.

global system, the state of freedom and democracy in it, and America's place in the world.

A Persistent Impulse

Throughout the centuries, global politics have been profoundly shaped by the successive iterations of a host of empires whose power, and whose territories, have waxed and waned with the geopolitical tides. That list includes the more-than sixteen dynasties that ruled China beginning in antiquity and stretching to the First World War. It also reflects the various iterations of the Russian empire, beginning in 1500 and stretching into the Soviet era. And it reflects the power and lasting impact of the three native empires of ancient Persia – the Achaemenid, the Parthian and the Sasanian – as well as more recent dynasties, from the Safavids (1501-1736) to the Pahlavis (1925-1979). In turn, these successive imperial iterations have helped create a clear worldview and identity on the part of Beijing, Moscow and Tehran that persists today.

In China, contemporary strategic culture – and imperial ambition – has been profoundly shaped by an extensive history of imperial conquest. According to the estimates of its own military, China waged close to 3,800 wars from 1100 BC to 1912.[2] It has also been informed by the conviction that China's imperial aspirations are legitimate, with the Middle Kingdom wielding the "mandate of heaven" to grow its territory, influence and power by any means necessary.

In Russia, today's renewed search for national greatness traces its roots back to the previously obscure school of thought known as Eurasianism. In the early 20th century, assorted thinkers propounded the necessity of a cultural and political struggle with the West. Today, those early ideas have been modernized into an absolutist, neo-fascist doctrine that asserts Russia's unique civilizational identity, its historical destiny as an empire, and the inevitability of conflict with an "Atlanticist" West.

---

2   As cited in Michael Sobolik, *Countering China's Great Game: A Strategy for American Dominance* (Annapolis: Naval Institute Press, 2024), 39.

For its part, Iran's imperial ideology has shifted dramatically over the past half-century. In prior eras, the exploits of Persian rulers like Cyrus and Darius became points of enormous pride, immortalized in books such as the poet Ferdowsi's 11th Century epic, *The Shahnameh*. In more recent centuries, robust nationalism – coupled with pre-Islamic traditions and practices – helped define an inclusive national identity. With the Islamic Revolution of 1979, however, these features were discarded in favor of an activist, militant Shi'ism. Yet the imperial urge that undergirded Persian expansionism has remained, although today it is imbued with a religious (even messianic) character.[3]

It should come as no surprise, therefore, that all three countries rank as revisionist states, and have consistently sought to alter the geopolitical *status quo* in their respective neighborhoods in their favor. Quite simply, they believe that they are both destined and entitled to do so – by dint of their past greatness, their current vision, and their future aspirations for global dominion.

The Drive for Empire, Modernized

Even so, the contemporary imperial impulses of China, Russia and Iran are qualitatively different from earlier iterations of the phenomenon in a number of ways.

First, they are *complementary*. With the notable exception of China's lingering claims to the eastern reaches of Russia, the territorial ambitions of the three are not in conflict with each another. Thus, Beijing's contemporary drive to expand its ambit in the Indo-Pacific does not affect Russian interests, nor do its claims over parts of Bhutan and India adversely affect Iran. In much the same way, Iran's persistent efforts to dominate the greater Middle East do not pose a challenge to the standing of either Russia or China in the region – and in fact afford them greater opportunity to pursue their own strategic objectives there. As for Russia's current war on Ukraine, as well as

---

3   See generally Ayatollah Ruhollah Khomeini (Joint Publication Research Service, trans.), *Islamic Government* (Manor Books, 1979).

the Kremlin's broader designs over the "post-Soviet space," both rebound to the benefit of Tehran and Beijing, insofar as the conflict has entangled Europe and the United States, giving the Islamic Republic and the PRC freer rein in their respective regions.

In historical terms, that constitutes a somewhat novel development. More often than not, empires that have coexisted at the same point in time have found themselves in conflict over territory, resources and political primacy. Prominent examples of this trend include the Ottoman conquest of Constantinople from the Byzantine Empire in 1453, and the more recent rupture between Nazi Germany and the USSR because of Adolph Hitler's designs over Soviet territory. By contrast, today's imperialists are defined by the complementarity of their claims, and by their willingness to work together to achieve them.

Second, they are *collaborative*. More and more, the international community is becoming aware of the deep, and deepening, connections that exist among China, Russia and Iran. Russian President Vladimir Putin and Chinese General Secretary Xi Jinping have, in recent years, built a "no limits" partnership that involves everything from military cooperation to coordination on disinformation and propaganda. Iran and China, meanwhile, have emerged as key enablers of Russia's war of aggression against Ukraine. The PRC, for its part, is playing an increasingly important role, both diplomatically and economically, in supporting the Islamic Republic of Iran in the face of both Western sanctions and widening regional disorder in the Middle East.

There is, of course, historical precedent for this. During the Second World War, Hitler's Germany, Mussolini's Italy and Hirohito's Japan also collaborated and coordinated policy in their attempts to annex new territories and dominate their respective regions of the world. Still, today's power dynamics among China, Russia and Iran are notable because modern technology adds significant complexity to the strategic challenge that each poses to the West.

Third, they are *absolutist*. It is commonly understood that empires inevitably seek to expand their borders outward, and the ambition to do so is often unbounded. From the Egyptians to the Mesopotamians to the Romans, the aspiration for global empire was ubiquitous. The Roman Empire was described in classical literature as extending "from the rising sun to the setting sun," and encompassing everything in between. In its modern form, the phrase was applied to the British Empire because of its colonial holdings in Africa, Asia and the Americas. Implicit in the expanding ambit of every empire has been the understanding that its rules, edicts and priorities would overwrite those that existed before the advent of conquest. However, this impulse was balanced against the need to preserve order in far-flung domains, and the real-world resource constraints of extended empire – all of which frequently led rulers (from the Romans to the Ottomans) to countenance a degree of political and ideological autonomy over territories that they claimed.

Fast forward to today, however, and it can be argued that the modern international environment has made such efforts more absolutist. A defining feature of today's imperialists, in other words, is that they share a desire to fundamentally undermine the existing global order and replace it with one more consonant with their wills, aspirations and political priorities. That, in turn, requires eroding sovereignty, reshaping identity and subjugating (by force if necessary) politically independent forces. Thus, China's vaunted Belt & Road Initiative (BRI), which for the past decade has served as Xi Jinping's signature foreign policy project, is best understood as an attempt to create an empire of dependency among the world's developing nations and bend them to Beijing's will. Russia's concept of "Novorossiya" – enshrined in official documents and popular literature alike – envisions the erasure not only of the Ukrainian state, but also of independent identity inconsistent with dominion by Moscow. As for Iran, the activist, radical strain of Shi'ism propounded by the Islamic Republic seeks to supplant other interpretations of the Muslim faith throughout the Middle East – and to undermine the authority of other nations, such as Saudi Arabia, which seek to guide it in a different direction.

The Challenge for America

For the United States, the shared imperial impulses of China, Russia and Iran constitute a cardinal challenge. At less than 250 years old, America is a comparatively young nation – one which to date has had comparatively little experience with imperial adversaries. Moreover, the United States now faces not one, not two, but three distinct imperial foes, each of which poses a challenge in its own right.

The central danger to American interests and U.S. primacy, however, stems from the ominous convergence of these forces. More and more, today's imperialists are helping one another to achieve their respective territorial conquests, through political assistance, economic support, the provision of military material, and assorted other means. But they are also coming together with a more ambitious goal: to remake the international environment in line with their visions and preferences.

The stakes could not be higher. If China's Xi Jinping, Russia's Vladimir Putin or Iran's Ali Khamenei succeed in imposing their wills on their respective regions, it would reshape those corners of the world to the profound detriment of the United States and its strategic partners there. But if Beijing, Moscow and Tehran manage to meaningfully alter the broader international order, the consequences could be truly global.

How should the United States and its allies respond to this new challenge? The pages that follow offer insights into the respective arcs of imperial history in Beijing, Moscow and Tehran. They also highlight just how much those arcs are, in the eyes of Chinese, Russian and Iranian policymakers, still incomplete and unfinished.

If they are allowed to persist unopposed, the consequences for the United States, for America's international allies, and for Western values writ large will be ruinous.

China: The Middle Kingdom on the March

In the Fall of 2013, Xi Jinping, newly installed as the General Secretary of the Chinese Communist Party, trekked to Astana, the capital of neighboring Kazakhstan, on a very public state visit. While there, he delivered what was perhaps the most important foreign policy address of his rule to date. Speaking at Nazarbayev University, named after the Central Asian republic's long-serving autocratic president, Xi highlighted a "golden opportunity" for development, and called for the revival of the Silk Road of antiquity.[4]

The speech marked the formal launch of what would come to be known as the Belt & Road Initiative (BRI), a sweeping economic and diplomatic offensive that, over the past dozen years, has come to dominate Chinese foreign policy and the PRC's relations with the "Global South." But Xi's address, replete with references to China's historical interests in Central Asia, was also a clear message that the country's imperial vision of its periphery was still very much alive.

That should not have been surprising. No other country in the world can match China's thousand-year history of imperialism. And today, under Xi's leadership, Beijing's appetite for territorial expansion is growing anew.

---

4   "Xi Jinping, Speech In Astana, Kazakhstan On Building A Silk Road Economic Belt With Central Asian Nations," University of Southern California USC US-China Institute, September 7, 2013, https://china.usc.edu/xi-jinping-speech-astana-kazakhstan-building-silk-road-economic-belt-central-asian-nations-september.

Internal Dynamics

To understand the true extent of Chinese imperialism, it is necessary to appreciate the full sweep of the Middle Kingdom's imperial conquest. Over the millennia, 56 ethnic groups were integrated into the successive dynasties that ruled over China. Today, those peoples still number some 105 million, or roughly 9 percent of the current population of the People's Republic of China.[5]

The status of these different ethnicities varies widely. Those that were absorbed into the power structures of dynastic China hundreds of years ago are by now so fully integrated that there may be only a few thousand left who speak their native language or abide by traditional customs. But those who currently face pressure from the PRC to fully assimilate still have millions of members who speak non-Chinese languages and hew to traditions that predate the modern Chinese state.

Tibet is a case in point. The region, which was ruled by successive Chinese empires in its early history, was reconquered by Beijing in 1950 and annexed into the fledgling PRC. Thereafter, the Chinese government launched an extensive campaign to subjugate and subordinate the region and its unique identity. The period of the Cultural Revolution saw many of the region's Buddhist monasteries destroyed by Mao Zedong's regime, while the decades since have witnessed Beijing continue its efforts to "sinicize" the region by obscuring its unique features and identifying markers. Language is prominent among these. Estimates of how many actually speak the main Tibetan languages vary widely, ranging from 1.3 million to as many as 6 million inhabitants. There is, however, far greater consensus about the locations where they are spoken: the Chinese regions of Tibet, Qinghai, Sichuan, Yunnan and Gansu, as well as (in lesser numbers) in neighboring countries, including Nepal, India and Bhutan.

Yet their numbers are unmistakably dwindling. Since Beijing's use of force to consolidate control over Tibet (first in 1950 and again in 1959), the practice of educating students in Mandarin, rather than the Tibetan language, has steadily reduced the numbers of Tibetans with fluency in their

---

5   "China," CIA *World Factbook*, 2022, https://www.cia.gov/the-world-factbook/countries/china/.

native tongue.[6] In this way, the PRC has helped to dilute Tibetan identity, dampen nationalistic tendencies among the region's population, and shift the frame of reference for Tibetans from one of historical distinctness to one in which they are simply one part of a larger political whole dominated by the CCP.

Xinjiang provides another example – albeit a much starker one. The region, conquered by the Qing Dynasty in the 18th century, held special status in the aftermath of the 1949 Chinese Civil War (a feature that was codified through a formal alteration of its name into the "Xinjiang Autonomous Region" in 1955). Until comparatively recently, the province enjoyed a degree of autonomy as a result of this arrangement. Over the past decade, however, the Chinese government has implemented an extensive campaign of repression in the province, seeking to "harmonize" it with the rest of the PRC by erasing defining ethnic features and subordinating what is seen as the inherently subversive practice of Islam in the once majority-Muslim region. According to widespread reporting, this policy has included: the mass internment and "reeducation" of the region's Uighur Muslims; widespread forced labor; extensive forced sterilizations; political indoctrination; and the wholesale suppression of Uighur religious practices.[7] So egregious has China's persecution of the Uighurs been that successive U.S. administrations, as well as a number of foreign governments, have termed it a "genocide."

Significantly, this heavy-handed imperialism has served a clear strategic purpose. In addition to "pacifying" an ethnic community that – because of its religious beliefs and distinct cultural traditions – is viewed with deep suspicion by Beijing, tightened control is imperative for another reason as well. It is a prerequisite for the smooth functioning of the Belt & Road,

---

6   See, for instance, Dong Zhe, "Can 'almost 100%' of Tibetans speak their ethnic language?" *Radio Free Asia*, August 31, 2023, https://www.rfa.org/english/news/afcl/fact-check-tibetan-08312023144305.html.

7   See, for instance, Lindsay Maizland, "China's repression of the Uighurs in Xinjiang," Council on Foreign Relations *Backgrounder*, September 22, 2022, https://www.cfr.org/backgrounder/china-xinjiang-uyghurs-muslims-repression-genocide-human-rights.

China's premier geopolitical and geo-economic project, owing to Xinjiang's strategic location as a gateway to Central and Southwest Asia.[8]

The Question of Taiwan

In the discussion of Chinese imperialism, there is no more pressing issue than that of Taiwan. While the issue has risen and fallen in importance for Chinese leaders in past years, today an increasingly assertive Beijing makes no secret of its desire to fully incorporate the island, as well as the more than 80 smaller islands under its jurisdiction, into the PRC. Indeed, China's contemporary elites believe unequivocally that reunification between the mainland and the island is an inevitability – and one that is likely to occur sooner rather than later. Thus, in his 2023 year-end address to the Chinese people, Xi himself argued that Taiwan's reabsorption was a "historical inevitability."[9]

Taiwan's importance to the Chinese leadership goes far beyond simple economic and political considerations. For many, the reincorporation of Taiwan into the PRC is a strategic and historical imperative, insofar as it would mark the definitive end of the country's civil war and the long-overdue unification of the Chinese people.

Here, the island's history plays a significant role. After centuries of self-rule and four decades as a colony of the Netherlands, China took control of Taiwan in the late 1600s and ruled the island until 1895 when, in the wake of the first Sino-Japanese war, it was occupied by Japan. In 1945, following Japan's defeat in the Second World War, the island was returned to Chiang Kai-shek's China. But the reunion proved short-lived; after his defeat at the hands of communist forces in the 1949 civil war, Chiang left mainland China for Taiwan, establishing a government in exile there (known as the Republic of China) from which he planned to stage an eventual return to power. At the same time, Mao Zedong's plans to invade Taiwan were

---

8   See, for instance, Michael Sobolik, statement before the House Select Committee on the Chinese Communist Party, May 16, 2024, https://www.afpc.org/uploads/documents/5-16_Select_Committee_CCP_Testimony_(Sobolik).pdf.

9   As cited in "China's Xi says 'reunification' with Taiwan is inevitable," Reuters, January 1, 2024, https://www.reuters.com/world/asia-pacific/china-calls-taiwan-president-frontrunner-destroyer-peace-2023-12-31/.

thwarted by deft American diplomacy – including the 1954 creation of the Southeast Asian Treaty Organization; the conclusion, in 1955, of a Mutual Defense Treaty between the United States and Taiwan; and Congress's 1955 "Formosa Resolution," which provided the U.S. president with broad authority to defend the island, should the need arise.

Chinese designs over Taiwan, moreover, were not constrained by diplomacy alone. Shows of American military force throughout the 1950s, including during the Taiwan Strait Crises of 1954-55 and 1958, had the effect of deterring the fledgling PRC from moving militarily against the island.[10] And President Dwight Eisenhower's 1958 decision to supply Taiwanese garrisons under attack led to a strange stability – namely, the PRC and the ROC (Taiwan) agreed to shell each other's garrisons on alternate days.[11] This arrangement would end up lasting for 20 years, until the PRC and United States normalized bilateral relations.

Since then, Taiwan has remained a perennial irritant in Sino-American ties, and the reassertion of PRC control over the island has been a persistent centerpiece of Chinese foreign policy. Moreover, under Xi, Beijing in recent years has exhibited growing boldness in altering the existing *status quo* surrounding the island. Crossings of the Taiwan Strait Median Line were essentially nonexistent for decades, before becoming a frequent occurrence (nearly 2,000 annually, on average) from 2020 onward.[12] At the same time, PLA incursions into Taiwan's Air Defense Identification Zone (ADIZ) have surged from some 380 in 2020 to over 1,700 a year since 2022.[13] The rise in military exercises near Taiwan is also concerning; significant, declared PLA

10   U.S. Department of State, Office of the Historian, "Milestones in the History of U.S. Foreign Relations," n.d., https://history.state.gov/milestones.

11   Ibid.

12   See, for instance, Cheng-kun Ma and K. Tristan Tang, "Military Implications of PLA Aircraft Incursions in Taiwan's Airspace 2024," Jamestown Foundation *China Brief* 25, iss. 1, January 17, 2025, https://jamestown.org/program/military-implications-of-pla-aircraft-incursions-in-taiwans-airspace-2024/.

13   William Langley, "PLA warplanes made a record 380 incursions into Taiwan's airspace in 2020, report says," *South China Morning Post*, January 6, 2021, https://www.scmp.com/news/china/military/article/3116557/pla-warplanes-made-record-380-incursions-taiwans-airspace-2020; Micah McCartney, "China Deployed Over 1,700 Military Planes Around Taiwan in 2023," *Newsweek*, January 5, 2024, https://www.newsweek.com/china-military-aircraft-taiwan-strait-2023-1858106.

military drills were rare prior to 2022, but have surged since as Beijing seeks to showcase (and to train) its military prowess vis-à-vis the island.[14]

Where is all this headed? In March 2024 testimony before the Senate Armed Services Committee, Admiral John Aquilino, the former head of U.S. Indo-Pacific Command (INDOPACOM), opined that "on a scale not seen since WWII, the PLA's buildup is occurring across land, sea, air, space cyber and information domains…"[15] The result is ominous; in Aquilino's assessment, "all indications point to the PLA meeting President Xi Jinping's directive to be ready to invade Taiwan by 2027."[16]

To be sure, "being ready" to invade is different from making a strategic decision to do so. However, given China's longstanding aim of reunification and its growing military capabilities (which would make it increasingly plausible for it to achieve such an outcome), prudence dictates that the United States needs to prepare for a worst-case scenario.

India: A Tense Border

China's imperial aspirations, however, extend far beyond Taiwan. The PRC has also staked extensive claims to parts of India's northern regions.

A protectorate during British colonial rule, Buddhist **Sikkum** (population 697,000) chose not to join the Indian Union after the British withdrew from the country in 1947. Subsequently, the 1950 Indo-Sikkim treaty restored the area's protectorate status, this time under the Republic of India. However, this status was not accepted by Beijing, and China's rejection of Sikkim's defined borders led to hundreds of casualties in the northern part of the province during India's 1962 war with the PRC, and subsequently to

---

14   See, for instance, Suyash Desai, "Forceful Taiwan Reunification: China's Targeted Military and Civilian-Military Measures," Foreign Policy Research Institute, March 11, 2025. https://www.fpri.org/article/2025/03/forceful-taiwan-reunification-chinas-targeted-military-and-civilian-military-measures/.

15   As cited in *Report of the Commission on the National Defense Strategy* (Santa Monica: RAND, July 2024), https://www.armed-services.senate.gov/imo/media/doc/nds_commission_final_report.pdf.

16   Ibid.

its parliament formally requesting to become part of the Indian Federation in 1975 – a move opposed at the time by China.[17]

Tensions between Beijing and New Delhi over the disposition of the territory have persisted since, occasionally flaring into open military skirmishes. Thus, 2017 saw a three-day stand-off between India and China following Indian objections to a Chinese road being built on the common border for the apparent reason of facilitating the movement of the Chinese army.[18] More recently, in January 2021, Chinese troops ventured across the border into Sikkim, and the resulting fighting left casualties on both sides.[19]

The 1914 Simla Accord signed by China, Tibet and Great Britain (as the colonial power ruling India), set the formal boundaries between India and imperial China. The repudiation of that treaty by the PRC provided the basis for Beijing's claim that India's northern province of **Arunachal Pradesh** (population of 1.4 million as of 2011) is rightly part of China. That claim contributed to India's 1962 war with the PRC and a series of subsequent skirmishes (the most recent of them in 2022) fought along Arunachal Pradesh's border with China.[20]

A clear statement of the Chinese position was issued in 2006 by then-Chinese Ambassador to India Sun Yuxi, who argued that "the whole of the state of Arunachal Pradesh is Chinese territory."[21] This assertion has provided the basis for China refusing visas to residents of Arunachal Pradesh, under the rationale that one does not need a visa to visit other parts of one's own country. In 2012, China chose to further proclaim its sovereignty over

---

17   U.S. Department of State, Office of the Historian, "Milestones in the History of U.S. Foreign Relations," n.d., https://history.state.gov/milestones.

18   U.S. Department of State, Office of the Historian, *Foreign Relations of the United States, 1969-1976*, Vol. E-8, https://history.state.gov/historicaldocuments/frus1969-76ve08; Sutirtho Patranobis, "'Should work together, fight Covid-19': China to India after Sikkim face-off," *Hindustan Times*, May 11, 2020, https://www.hindustantimes.com/india-news/should-work-together-fight-covid-19-china-to-india-after-sikkim-face-off/story-jfIylTI1T71y1TLfFutWAN.html.

19   See, for instance, "Sikkim: Chinese and Indian troops 'in new border clash,'" *BBC*, January 25, 2021, https://www.bbc.com/news/world-asia-55793112#.

20   See, for instance, Gerry Shih, "Indian and Chinese soldiers battle in latest high-altitude clash at border," *Washington Post*, December 13, 2022, https://www.washingtonpost.com/world/2022/12/12/india-china-arunachal-border/.

21   "Arunachal Pradesh is our territory: Chinese envoy," *Rediff*, November 14, 2006, https://www.rediff.com/news/2006/nov/14china.htm.

Arunachal Pradesh by issuing passports with a map showing these territories as part of its territory.[22]

The end of China's 1962 war with India saw 14,672 square miles of India (the "Western Sector") surrendered to the PRC. However, Chinese territorial ambitions in India's North did not subside, and the PRC formally claims an additional 580 square miles of **Ladakh**, 116 square miles in **Himachal Pradesh** and 702 square miles in **Uttarakhand**. Indeed, maps in new Chinese passports show these areas as part of China.[23] Unsurprisingly, tensions have persisted along these border areas, and sporadic clashes have occurred there – albeit largely without the loss of life.[24]

Bullying Bhutan

A tiny Buddhist nation of 782,000 people nestled between India and China, Bhutan is likewise the target of Chinese imperial designs.[25] With Great Britain's withdrawal from the country in 1949 and India's subsequent declaration of independence, New Delhi assumed responsibility for protecting Bhutan from external threats. However, this did not mark an end to Chinese claims on its territory. Efforts to settle those claims resulted in Bhutan's ceding of 154 square miles of land (known as Kula Khari) to Beijing in the 1980s. However, as of 2015, eight areas – totaling approximately 300 square miles – remain in dispute. That year, China constructed an entirely new village in the disputed territory to go along with infrastructure previously erected there.[26]

---

22 "India and China row over new map in passport," *BBC*, November 23, 2012, https://www.bbc.com/news/world-asia-india-20459064.

23 Max Fisher, "Here's the Chinese passport map that's infuriating much of Asia," *Washington Post*, November 26, 2012, https://www.washingtonpost.com/news/worldviews/wp/2012/11/26/heres-the-chinese-passport-map-thats-infuriating-much-of-asia/.

24 A notable exception took place in 2022, when 20 Indians died as a result of clashes with Indian forces. Krishn Kaushik, "Indian, Chinese troops clashed twice in 2022 even as peace talks were on," Reuters, January 17, 2024, https://www.reuters.com/world/asia-pacific/indian-chinese-troops-clashed-twice-2022-even-peace-talks-were-2024-01-17/#:~:text=NEW%20DELHI%2C%20Jan%2017%20 (Reuters,Indian%20Army's%20gallantry%20award%20citations).

25 United States Indo-Pacific Command, "Topic: Border Dispute Between China and Bhutan," USINDOPACOM J06/SJA TACAID Series, March 11, 2024, https://www.pacom.mil/Portals/55/Documents/Legal/J06%20TACAID%20-%20PRC-BHUTAN%20BORDER%20DISPUTE%20 (FINAL).pdf?ver=ofbfrNNgIqZr7nFqm60lbw%3D%3D.

26 Robert Barnett, "China Is Building Entire Villages in Another Country's Territory," *Foreign Policy*, May 7, 2021, https://foreignpolicy.com/2021/05/07/china-bhutan-border-villages-security-forces/.

Recent years have seen stepped-up efforts by Thimphu to peacefully resolve the issue. This included discussions in 2023 between Bhutan's Foreign Minister, Tandi Dorji, and Chinese Foreign Minister Wang Yi. But while those diplomatic contacts saw expressions of support from Beijing for a settlement of outstanding boundary claims,[27] no solution to the problem has yet been found.

A Widening Ambit in the Indo-Pacific

To the extent that it has not already done so, the PRC also seeks to establish *de facto* control over islands that are concurrently claimed by Brunei, Malaysia, and the Philippines (as well as Taiwan, and Vietnam). Chinese interests, once defined by its widely known "nine-dash line," were expanded in 2023 with the issuance of a ten-dash line that further broadened Beijing's already-extensive regional claims.[28]

China and **the Philippines** advance conflicting historical claims over the sovereignty of islands in the South China Sea (which is called the West Philippine Sea by Manila). In January 2013, pursuant to the United Nations Convention on the Law of the Sea (UNCLOS), to which both the Philippines and the PRC are signatories, the Philippines initiated an international arbitration to challenge Chinese claims over the Spratly Islands and Scarborough Shoal.[29] China declined to participate in the arbitration, and has ignored the arbitral tribunal's subsequent July 2016 decision in favor of the Philippines on most of its counts.[30] As a result, both sides continue to pursue their claims – China by force and the Philippines through diplomacy.

The most hotly contested areas in this regard are Scarborough Shoal,

27 "China aims to establish diplomatic relations with Bhutan soon: FM," Xinhua, October 23, 2023, https://english.news.cn/20231023/c2070abd8cec441c8e4df6504dcad463/c.html.

28 Troy Clayman, "China's New Map: The 10-Dash Line," *The Boston Political Review*, December 22, 2023, https://www.bostonpoliticalreview.org/post/china-s-new-map-the-10-dash-line; Colin Clark, "New Chinese 10-Dash map sparks furor across Indo-Pacific: Vietnam, India, Philippines, Malaysia," *Breaking Defense*, September 1, 2023, https://breakingdefense.com/2023/09/new-chinese-10-dash-map-sparks-furor-across-indo-pacific-vietnam-india-philippines-malaysia/.

29 Permanent Court of Arbitration, "The South China Sea Arbitration (The Republic of the Philippines v. The People's Republic of China," Case 2013-19, n.d., https://pca-cpa.org/es/cases/7/#:-:text=On%2022%20January%202013%2C%20the,(the%20"Convention").

30 Ibid.

Thitu, and Mischief Reef. At its closest point, Scarborough Shoal lies 120 miles west of the Philippine Island of Luzon and 450 miles east of China's Hainan Island. In July 2012, Beijing built a barrier to the entrance of the Shoal and began the practice, which continues to this day, of turning away Filipino vessels. Practically speaking, China now controls the Shoal. The tiny Spratly island of Thitu, meanwhile, has been home to Philippine residents since the 1970s. The island lies 486 nautical miles from China's Hainan Island, and 270 nautical miles from Philippine territory. The several hundred Filipinos that currently live there deal with harassment from Chinese Coast guard ships, which regularly force fisherman away from their preferred fishing grounds. Finally, Mischief Reef, a part of the Spratly Islands, lies 129 nautical miles west of the Philippines and 599 nautical miles east of Hainan Island. It was the site of a ninety-minute battle between a Philippine navy gunboat and Chinese naval assets in January 1996.[31] China exercises *de facto* control over the reef, on which it has reclaimed land and built a military base.[32]

The small monarchy of **Brunei**, with a population of 449,000, has not actively pursued its claim to three features in its Exclusive Economic Zone (EEZ)[33]: Louisa Reef, Owen Shoal and Rifleman Bank. Neither, however, has it abandoned them. Additionally, the space between the 5th and 6th dashes of China's "nine-dash line" come within 35 nautical miles of Brunei's coast. For its part, China has as yet made no efforts to consolidate these claims, which lie approximately 1100 miles from its nearest internationally recognized land feature (Hainan Island).

Malaysia contests China's claim to sovereignty over 10 southern Spratly features. The best known are Swallow Reef, Ardaiser Reef, Erica Reef, Mariveles Reef and Investigator Shoal. By a factor of two, these features are much closer to Malaysia than they are to China. For instance,

---

31 Council on Foreign Relations, "China's Maritime Disputes," n.d., https://www.cfr.org/timeline/chinas-maritime-disputes.

32 Hannah Beech, "China's Sea Control Is a Done Deal, 'Short of War With the U.S.,'" *New York Times*, September 20, 2018, https://www.nytimes.com/2018/09/20/world/asia/south-china-sea-navy.html.

33 Under international law, and Exclusive Economic Zone is a maritime zone that extends up to 200 miles from a country's coastline, where the nation in question enjoys sovereign (but not necessarily exclusive) rights over commerce, resource exploitation, and conservation activities.

Investigator Shoal is situated 376 miles from Malaysia's Sabah, and 841 miles from China's Hainan Island. Especially around those features, near suspected or proven oil deposits, Malaysia maintains a military presence. As in other contested parts of the Spratlys, China has made a practice of sending ships through Malaysia's EEZ. Formal Malay protests were made after aggressive PRC actions in 2018 and 2021.[34] In the 2020s, PRC ships, including China's largest Coast Guard craft, began repeated aggressive behavior against Malay vessels.[35]

China and **Vietnam** each claim the entirety of both the Paracel and Spratly Islands. Since its defeat of Hanoi at the January 1974 Battle of the Paracel Islands, however, Beijing has exercised full control over the Paracels. The 100 reefs, atolls and islands of the Spratlys are scattered over 158,000 square miles. The Philippines, Taiwan, Brunei and Malaysia also claim part or all of the Spratlys, but the struggle between Vietnam and China is, by far, the most intense. In the 1970s, three of the Spratlys were occupied by Vietnam ahead of a threatened Chinese occupation.[36] Following bloody clashes in March of 1988 in which 64 mostly unarmed Vietnamese were killed, Beijing gained control of Johnson South, a Spratly Island reef. China's aggressive behavior accelerated between 2013 and 2015, when its island-building in the Spratlys created approximately 3,000 acres of land that now contain military bases.[37] However, Chinese island building slowed following its 2014 deployment of an oil rig 80 miles inside of Vietnam's EEZ – a move resulting in a stand-off that led to the sinking of a Vietnamese boat and large violent anti-Chinese protests in Vietnam.[38] Since 2019, tensions have risen as a result of accelerating Chinese patrols in Vietnam's EEZ, especially in those areas that are rich in oil and gas. The Vietnamese response, beginning

---

34 "Malaysia summons Chinese envoy to protest South China Sea incursion," *The Straits Times*, October 5, 2021, https://www.straitstimes.com/asia/se-asia/malaysia-summons-chinese-envoy-to-protest-south-china-sea-incursion.

35 Rebecca Tan, "Malaysia's appetite for oil and gas puts it on a collision course with China," *Washington Post*, May 11, 2024, https://www.washingtonpost.com/world/2024/05/11/china-malaysia-south-china-sea/.

36 National Bureau of Asian Research, Maritime Awareness Project, "Country Profile: Vietnam," n.d., https://www.nbr.org/publication/vietnam/.

37 Rebecca Tan and Laris Karklis, "Vietnam accelerates island building to challenge China's maritime claims," *Washington Post*, August 9, 2024, https://www.washingtonpost.com/world/interactive/2024/vietnam-south-china-sea-islands-growth/.

38 Ibid.

in 2021, was an intense "island building" campaign that expanded by ten-fold the area of land on Spratly rocks, reefs and islets claimed by Vietnam.[39] In 2024 alone, Vietnam was estimated to be on track to create more than 1,000 acres of new land.[40]

A Tense Relationship with Tokyo

Centuries of contradictory historical claims fuel competing – and acri-monious – Chinese and Japanese assertions of sovereignty over the five uninhabited islands and three reefs that constitute the Senkaku/Diaoyu Islands. However, it is clear that Japan controlled the islands between 1895 and 1945, and the U.S. subsequently administered them between 1945 and 1972. Though the U.S. returned control of the area to Japan in 1972, the 1960 Japanese-American Treaty of Mutual Cooperation and Security still obligates Washington to defend the islands against foreign aggression. This has created a potential flashpoint between Washington and Beijing.

Indeed, on June 9, 2016, a Chinese navy frigate entered the island's (and therefore Japan's) contiguous zone[41] *en route* to its territorial waters – a first for a Chinese naval vessel.[42] After initially refusing the Japanese request to leave, diplomatic efforts succeeded in convincing the ship to depart before entering territorial waters.[43] Such Chinese brinksmanship has contributed to the deepening defense cooperation between Japan and Vietnam, as well as between Japan and the Philippines.

---

39   Ibid.

40   Ibidem.

41   Under the Law of the Sea Treaty, a contiguous zone may extend up to 24 nautical miles from a country's coastline.

42   Todd Hall, "More Significance than Value: Explaining Developments in the Sino-Japanese Contest Over the Senkaku/Diaoyu Islands," *Texas National Security Review* 2, iss. 4, September 2019, https://tnsr.org/2019/09/more-significance-than-value-explaining-developments-in-the-sino-japanese-contest-over-the-senkaku-diaoyu-islands/.

43   Ibid.

Persistent Designs Over The Russian Far East

No list of China's existing territorial claims and aspirations would be complete without a mention of the largest areas of land coveted by China – albeit abstractly, for the moment. Those are parts of Eastern Siberia and the Russian Far East, a land mass roughly equivalent to that of Western Europe.

The history is fraught. Exploiting China's weakness following the Second Opium War (1856-1860), Russia seized these territories, something which remained a bone of contention between the two countries for decades. Indeed, in previous years, official Chinese maps have depicted large swathes of the Russian Far East as being "Chinese territories invaded and occupied by Tsarist Russia," suggesting ongoing Chinese desires for a restoration of these lands. [44]

That is only a remote possibility, at least for the time being. The current high level of cooperation with Russia, and Russia's nuclear capability, makes it highly unlikely that the PRC will aggressively try to reclaim these lands. However, since these lands are sparsely populated and poor, Chinese immigration and economic penetration may well be used as a first step toward a full integration of these territories into China – a step that a future Russia may be unwilling or unable to resist.

Imperialism and Chinese Ideology

While Western policymakers have only become focused on them in recent years, Beijing's current imperial aspirations are far from new. Rather, they are the contemporary manifestation of longstanding ideas, beliefs and convictions that cumulatively make up Chinese strategic culture. Over the past decade, these tenets have become weaponized under the guidance of Xi Jinping into an increasingly aggressive, expansionist official foreign policy line.

At the center of China's current imperial impulse is the deeply held belief, hearkening back to imperial times, that the country is destined to rule over *tianxia*, or "all under heaven." Notably, that concept began as a

---

44   See Herman Pirchner, Jr. *The Russian-Chinese Border: Today's Reality* (AFPC, August 2002), 9.

corrective to the vulnerabilities that plagued the ancient Chinese state. As the scholar Michael Sobolik has explained:

> In its infancy, China lacked natural borders to guard its vaunted civilization. There was broad recognition that security demanded buffer zones in all directions. Bulwarks took multiple forms, either natural or man-made. Some were defensive, like the Great Wall; many others, as we will see, were offensive. Power, not security, was the overriding logic behind *tianxia*.[45]

Over time, however, the idea has evolved and expanded along with Chinese power, rooted in a selective reading of history that placed the Middle Kingdom at the center of global affairs. China came to see itself as the "sole sovereign government of the world," as well as "the center of its own hierarchical and theoretically universal concept of world order," noted Henry Kissinger in his 2014 book *World Order*.[46]

In modern times, the Chinese Communist Party has become the natural inheritor of this mandate. For decades, however, *tianxia* receded as an organizing strategic concept, as successive Chinese leaders in the post-Mao Zedong-era prioritized the country's "peaceful rise." During these years (spanning the late 1970s to the early 2010s), the PRC worked to insinuate itself into the existing world order so as to most effectively benefit from it. The effort was wildly successful. By the early 2000s, policymakers in Washington had become convinced that China was steadily becoming a "responsible stakeholder" in the prevailing global order.[47]

Not so now. Under Xi Jinping, China has reverted to imperial thinking that sees China as the legitimate inheritor of the world – and ascribes diminished sovereignty to all other nations. For instance, Xi's signature foreign policy project, the BRI, is more often than not depicted in over-

45 Sobolik, *Countering China's Great Game*, 31.
46 As cited in Gordon G. Chang, *Plan Red: China's Project to Destroy America* (West Palm Beach: Humanix, 2024), 10.
47 See, for instance, Robert B. Zoellick, remarks before the National Committee on U.S.-China Relations, New York City, September 21, 2005, https://2001-2009.state.gov/s/d/former/zoellick/rem/53682.htm.

whelmingly economic terms, as simply a sprawling web of infrastructure and development projects throughout the Global South. It is indeed that; since its launch in 2013, the BRI has become a truly colossal national undertaking, with an estimated total value of more than $1 trillion and projects in close to 150 nations around the world.[48] It has succeeded in establishing the PRC as the lender of first resort and an indispensable partner for much of the developing world. Yet, as numerous studies have highlighted, it is impossible to fully account for the project solely in economic terms. Rather, the preponderance of the evidence suggests that the BRI represents an effort by the PRC to establish an empire of dependence with itself at the center.

While a comprehensive study of the BRI lies outside the scope of its work, the ideological underpinnings that animate it are not. Indeed, they track closely with the territorial aspirations and expansionist ambitions detailed in the preceding pages. In multiple ways, Xi's China has effectively modernized the concept of *tianxa*, articulating a global vision that is opposed to, and fundamentally in tension with, the established Western-led world order. Or, as Sobolik puts it, "Xi Jinping's goal is striking similar to the ambitions of his dynastic predecessors: the recognition from all under heaven that China is superior."[49]

48   Christoph Nedopil Wang, "China Belt and Road Initiative (BRI) Investment Report 2024," FISF Fudan University, Green Finance & Development Center, February 27, 2025, https://greenfdc.org/china-belt-and-road-initiative-bri-investment-report-2024/; Christoph Nedopil, "China Belt and Road Initiative (BRI) Investment Report 2022," FISF Fudan University, Green Finance & Development Center, January 2023, https://greenfdc.org/wp-content/uploads/2023/02/Nedopil-2023_China-Belt-and-Road-Initiative-BRI-Investment-Report-2022.pdf.

49   Sobolik, *Countering China's Great Game*, 43.

Russia: Renewed dreams of Eurasian empire

In the early morning hours of February 24, 2022, Russian President Vladimir Putin formally renewed his 2014 invasion of Ukraine. For most, the offensive – characterized by the Kremlin as a "special military operation" – came as a near-total surprise. For weeks, Western observers had been making the case that, despite mounting evidence of a massive Russian buildup along the country's common border with Ukraine, Russia's strongman president was not actually serious about invading his country's western neighbor. What these analysts, and numerous others, neglected to take into account was a fundamental variable: the indispensable role that Ukraine occupies in the Russian imperial imagination. It was this role that made Moscow's attempt at conquest inevitable and ultimately drove Putin's war of choice.

In the weeks and months leading up to his fateful decision, Russia's president had been communicating precisely this point. In July of 2021, Putin published a long treatise on the official Kremlin website laying out the case for the "historical unity" of Russians and Ukrainians. Putin's article argued that "the idea of Ukrainian people as a nation separate from the Russians" was a concept that had been promoted by foreign elites, emphasized that "Ukraine and Russia have developed as a single economic system over decades and centuries," and posited that Ukraine's current, diminished role on the world stage was a product of its present distance from Moscow.[50] Russia's president, in other words, was laying the intellectual groundwork

---

50   Office of the President of Russia, "Article by Vladimir Putin "On the Historical Unity of Russians and Ukrainians,"" July 12, 2021, http://en.kremlin.ru/events/president/news/66181.

for a new imperial push to reabsorb Ukraine, despite the latter's decades of post-Soviet independence.

The idea was hardly novel. Imperial ideology has long dominated the thinking of Russia's elites. As the historian Orlando Figes has noted, "Between 1500 and the revolution of 1917, the Russian Empire grew at an astonishing rate, 130 square kilometres [50 square miles] on average every day."[51] Nor, apart from its scope, was the expansionist ideology undergirding these imperial successes unique to Russian elites during those years. England, France, Italy, Belgium, Germany and other nation-states also pursued imperial ambitions by force.

Still, Moscow's continued embrace of imperial ideology is unique among Europe's major powers. Today, in the context of Russia's foreign policy, it possesses three major strains.

Reviving Greater Russia

The first of these characteristics stems from a deep-seated conviction across the national political spectrum that Russians, Belarussians, and Ukrainians must be united into a Greater Slavic State. Famed anti-communist icon Alexander Solzhenitsyn advanced this idea in his later years, following the collapse of the Soviet Union.[52] So, too, did Russia's one-time Deputy Prime Minister, Dmitri Rogozin. In his 2003 book, tellingly entitled *We Will Reclaim Russia for Ourselves,* Rogozin wrote:

...the lack of understanding of the Russian question, the division of the Russian nation gives us the feeling of an unrepaid debt. And debts must be repaid. Russians... should discuss out loud the problem of a divided people that has an historic right to political unification of its own land. We (Russians) must present ourselves with the problem of a union, no matter how unrealistic this idea is in today's conditions. And we must create conditions to result

---

51   Orlando Figes, *The Story of Russia* (Metropolitan Books, 2022), 1835.

52   Herman Pirchner, Jr., *Reviving Greater Russia: The Future of Russia's Borders with Belarus, Georgia, Kazakhstan, Moldova and Ukraine* (University Press of America, 2005).

in the environment with which Germany dealt for forty years coming out united in the end.[53]

A recent target of this enduring fixation has been **Ukraine** – and for good reason. As Putin himself has laid out in detail,[54] Ukraine occupies a unique place in the imperial history of Russia. It is consequently an integral component of any future planned Russian expansion.

The modern Ukrainian state traces its beginnings to the state of Kyivan Rus, which, until its conquest by the Mongols in the 13th Century, was geographically the largest state in Europe. Following the Mongol withdrawal from the territory of what is present-day Ukraine, most of it was ruled until 1795 by the Polish-Lithuanian Commonwealth.[55] Thereafter, the politically unsettled aftermath of Russia's defeat in the First World War and the subsequent Bolshevik revolution permitted national independence for a time. But by 1921, part of Ukraine's west came under the rule of a newly independent Poland, while its center and east became part of the USSR. Full Soviet control of Ukraine followed World War II and persisted until the USSR's collapse in 1991, whereupon Ukraine gained independence anew.

That control was both protracted and brutal. Its seminal event was the man-made famine known as the Holodomor. Orchestrated by Soviet authorities as a way of suppressing opposition to the USSR on the part of the Ukrainian peasantry, the policy – entailing collective punishment as a result of low crop yields – is estimated to have resulted in the death of between 5-7 million Ukrainians in 1932-1933 in what many countries (including the United States) have recognized as a genocide.[56]

This history is instructive in understanding Ukraine's intense opposition to both the 2014 and 2022 Russian invasions. Having survived centuries of occupation and repression, especially during the Soviet era, Ukrainian culture and language have evolved into a clear and cohesive sense of identity,

53   Ibid.

54   Office of the President of Russia, "Article by Vladimir Putin 'On the Historical Unity of Russians and Ukrainians.'"

55   The exception is lands that were taken by Czarist Russia in 1654, 1772 and 1793.

56   For a detailed history of the Holodomor, see Anne Applebaum, *Red Famine: Stalin's War on Ukraine* (Toronto: Signal/McClelland & Stewart, 2017).

as well as the desire to live free of Moscow's heavy yoke. That orientation is central to the dogged fight that Ukraine has been waging for years.

But if Ukraine seeks freedom from Russian domination, Moscow is equally committed to the country's reconquest – by various means. Following its 1991 independence, Ukraine saw mounting attempts at political subversion emanating from Moscow, as Russia gradually regained its geopolitical strength and global stature. Russian consulates in Eastern Ukraine and Crimea funded and organized pro-Russian elements in Ukrainian society, and their efforts were part of the reason that pro-Kremlin politician Viktor Yanukovich succeeded in winning the Ukrainian presidency in 2010. Yanukovich's subsequent efforts to buck the will of the people and move his country closer to Moscow led to widespread discontent, culminating in the 2014 "Revolution of Dignity" that drove him from power.

In the chaotic aftermath of Yanukovich's flight to Russia (where he still lives as of this writing), Russia's military moved to take control of the Crimean Peninsula and later to invade parts of Eastern Ukraine. However, Ukrainian volunteers rallied to limit the scope of that invasion to segments of the Ukrainian provinces of Luhansk and Donetsk. And, in spite of periodic skirmishes, these forces succeeded in maintaining that line of control until the full-scale Russian invasion of February 24, 2022.

That Russia used a 2001 "Law on the Expansion of the Russian Federation" as the legal basis to annex Crimea is a testament to the fact that Russia's imperial aims were in motion long before 2014. In turn, the Kremlin's ultimate objective in Ukraine has been made clear by no less senior a figure than Deputy Security Council Chairman (and former President) Dmitri Medvedev. "One of the former leaders of Ukraine once said that Ukraine is not Russia," Medvedev argued publicly in March 2024. "This concept needs to disappear once and for all. Ukraine is without a doubt Russia."[57]

Ukraine is not alone. A second object of Russia's immediate imperial longing is neighboring **Belarus**. That country has a history of foreign rule, first by Kyivan Rus (beginning in the 9th Century), then by Lithuania

---

57   Dmitry Medvedev, speech before the World Youth Festival 2024, March 4, 2024, https://fest2024.com/en/news/dmitrij-medvedev-chuzhoj-zemli-nam-ne-nado-no-ot-svoego-my-ne-otstupimsya-nikogda.

(starting in 1240), thereafter by the confederation of Poland and the Grand Duchy of Lithuania (commencing in 1385), and still later by the Polish-Lithuanian Commonwealth (from 1565 on). Czarist Russia subsequently acquired virtually all the territory of contemporary Belarus through the three partitions of Poland (which took place in 1772, in 1793, and in 1795).

So the situation persisted until after World War I, when most of today's Belarus was briefly ruled by Germany and the Soviet Union, before being divided into three parts pursuant to the 1921 Treaty of Riga. That agreement gave the Western part of present-day Belarus to Poland, and the remainder to two separate parts of the USSR. Subsequently, in 1939, the Soviet Union, then an ally of Nazi Germany, facilitated the German capture of Belarusian territories held by Poland. Thereafter, in 1944, the Soviets – by then adversaries of Hitler's Third Reich – recaptured Belarus and ruled it until the 1991 Soviet collapse enabled it to emerge as an independent state.

Quickly, however, Russia began working to erode Belarusian independence – a process that culminated in the December 1999 Treaty on the Creation of a Union State of Russia and Belarus. As its name implied, that agreement envisioned a political, strategic and economic union of the two countries. In August 2002, shortly after his rise to power, Russian President Vladimir Putin sought to formalize such an arrangement through a referendum on a formal merger that was to be held in both countries the following year. But, as a result of resistance from Minsk, such a vote was never held. Nevertheless, Minsk has gradually become more and more economically and militarily integrated with Moscow. Over the years, Russian and Belarusian troops have held joint exercises and, with Minsk's approval, Russian troops used Belarusian territory as a staging ground for their 2022 invasion of Ukraine. In varying numbers, the Russian military has remained in Belarus ever since, and it is not at all clear that Moscow's forces will leave once the current war has concluded.

Finally, there is **northern Kazakhstan**. Russia's presence in the country began in the mid 1700s, when the Kazakhs sought Russian support against the Oyrats, as the westernmost group of Mongols were known. After the Oyrats were exterminated by the Manchurian Chinese in the late

1750s, Russia began to establish a military presence on Kazakh territory and encourage its own citizens to move there. Integration was not seamless, however. An estimated 25% or more of the Kazakh population died because of revolts or famine during the takeover before the country finally became a Soviet Socialist Republic in 1936.[58] The last bloody repression occurred during World War I, with an estimated 150,000 Kazakh killed and another 200,000 fleeing to China.[59]

With the collapse of the Soviet Union in 1991, Kazakhstan became fully independent. But it was not fully unified, owing to its diverse ethnic makeup: only 40 percent of the population was Kazakh, while 38 percent was Russian, 5 percent was Ukrainian, and the remaining 17 percent was a mixture of other nationalities.[60] Since then, however, those proportions have shifted considerably as a result of disparate birthrates, emigration and other factors. As of 2022, 71 percent of the population was Kazakh, 15 percent was Russian, and 14 percent represented other nationalities.[61] The remaining Russian population of Kazakhstan is concentrated in parts of the country that border Russia, including the industrial hub of East Kazakhstan. It is this territory that proponents of a Greater Slavic State hope to return to Russia's control.

That impulse, in turn, is a source of abiding worry for officials in Astana. Presumably concerned that a Russian victory over Ukraine would strengthen Russian nationalists who wish to take Kazakh territory, President Kassym-Jomart Tokayev told Putin in a public meeting at the June 2022 St. Petersburg International Economic Forum that his country remained committed to the principle of territorial integrity and would not recognize the quasi-states of Donetsk and Luhansk.[62] That caused Russian parliamen-

---

58 See, for instance, Mark B. Tauger, "Modernisation in Soviet Agriculture," in Markku Kangaspuro and Jeremy Smith, eds., *Modernisation in Russia since 1900* (Studia Fennica Historica, 2006).

59 S.K. Narottam, "Politics of Nation-Building and State-Formation in Kazakhstan," *Pakistan Horizon* 59, iss. 3, April 2006, https://www.jstor.org/stable/41394126.

60 Appendix (Table 6) in G. Baratova et al., eds. *History of Kazakhstan – Peoples and Cultures* (Almaty: Daik Press, 2001), 596-597.

61 "Country Summary: Kazakhstan," *CIA World Factbook*, 2024.

62 Marie Dumulin, "Steppe change: How Russia's war on Ukraine is reshaping Kazakhstan," European Council on Foreign Relations, April 13, 2023, https://ecfr.eu/publication/steppe-change-how-russias-war-on-ukraine-is-reshaping-kazakhstan/.

tarian Konstantin Zatulin to warn Kazakhstan, "if we have friendship… then no territorial questions are raised. But if that does not exist, everything is possible… as in the case of Ukraine."[63] In the same spirit, a since-deleted social media post by Dmitry Medvedev suggested that, after Ukraine, northern Kazakhstan might be next.[64]

Significantly, this drive for a Greater Slavic State is also guided by more practical considerations. Namely, it has the power to serve, at least for a time, as a corrective for Russia's protracted demographic decline. For more than half a century, Russia has been locked in a cycle of deepening population downturn, with death and emigration significantly outpacing live births. The situation became a full-blown crisis in the decade after the collapse of the USSR, before rebounding modestly to European levels of fertility.[65] This situation continues to prevail today, despite numerous Kremlin initiatives designed to boost birth rates. Moreover, it has been greatly exacerbated by Russia's war on Ukraine, as ideological objectors, political opponents, and those simply seeking to avoid conscription have sought the shelter of other nations. As the *Washington Post* noted in February of 2023, the war has touched off a "historic exodus" of Russians from the country, one unrivaled in size and scope since the 1917 Bolshevik Revolution.[66] All of which has significantly worsened Russia's already grim demographic prospects. It has also helped reinforce to Russian officials the strategic logic behind their reinvigorated drive for a Greater Slavic State.

---

63   Ibid.

64   Temur Umarov, "After Ukraine, Is Kazakhstan Next in the Kremlin's Sights?" Carnegie Endowment for International Peace *Politika*, August 10, 2022, https://carnegieendowment.org/russia-eurasia/politika/2022/08/after-ukraine-is-kazakhstan-next-in-the-kremlins-sights?lang=en.

65   Notably, Russia's fertility rate – like that of the entirety of Europe – still falls significantly below the 2.1 live births per woman needed for a stable replacement of national populations. As of 2023, Europe's average fertility rate was just 1.38. "Fertility statistics," Eurostat, February 2025, https://ec.europa.eu/eurostat/statistics-explained/index.php. The same year, Russia's fertility rate was 1.41. "Russia's fertility rate is 'catastrophically low,'" *IntelliNews*, July 29, 2024, https://www.intellinews.com/russia-s-fertility-rate-is-catastrophically-low-335864/.

66   Francesca Ebel and Mary Ilyushina, "Russians abandon wartime Russia in historic exodus," *Washington Post*, February 13, 2023, https://www.washingtonpost.com/world/2023/02/13/russia-diaspora-war-ukraine/.

A Russia-Dominated Sphere

The second strain of Russia's imperial impulse has focused on the idea of recreating a sphere of extended strategic influence along the country's periphery. This, policymakers in Moscow believe, is not only a prerequisite for renewed national greatness. It is a necessity because of the encroachment of Western values, principles and norms that are seen as deeply subversive by the Kremlin. These convictions have led Russian officials to seek to reconstitute the national boundaries that prevailed for much of the preceding century.

In practical terms, this has meant calls for the annexation of some Christian parts of the former Soviet Union (for example, Moldova, Georgia, and the Baltic states) as well as the establishment of a Moscow-dominated sphere of influence in the non-Muslim parts that were formerly part of the Czarist empire (including Poland and Finland). Annexation of these territories, if it can feasibly be achieved, is also the stated goal of some in the Kremlin's corridors of power.[67] Thus, in a September 2023 interview with the state-run RIA Novosti news agency, Yevgany Balitsky, who at the time was the man overseeing the Russian-occupied Ukrainian territory of Zaporizhzhia, outlined that:

> When the Russian Empire faltered after the Bolshevik coup and took a different development path, it lost many of its territories… this included Warsaw, Helsinki, Revel, Liepaja and the entire Baltic States… We must correct this.[68]

The lost lands referred to by Balitsky include **Latvia and Estonia**, which share a long history of Russian domination. From the 13th Century until the early 18th, both were ruled by either Germans, Danes, Poles, Swedes, or the Polish-Lithuanian Empire. Subsequently, the 1710 defeat of Sweden by Czar Peter the Great kicked off two centuries of Russian rule – a rule

---

67   See, for instance, Andrew Osborn and Caleb Davis, "Medvedev floats idea of pushing back Poland's borders," Reuters, February 24, 2023, https://www.reuters.com/world/europe/russias-medvedev-floats-idea-pushing-back-polandsborders-2023-02-24/.

68   As cited in Alisa Orlova, "Kremlin Official Openly Calls For 'Return' of Baltic States Using 'Russian Weapons,'" *Kyiv Post*, October 4, 2023, https://www.kyivpost.com/post/22302?gsid=6e552432-204e-4ad3-ae58-2679f677d730.

that was aided by the active cooperation of local German nobility. Following the Bolshevik revolution and the end of World War I, Estonia and Latvia established their independence through a 15-month war (1918-1920) against both Russian Bolshevik and Baltic German forces. That independence lasted until 1940, when Soviet forces briefly occupied their territory before being pushed out in June 1941 – only to regain control some three years later, in 1944. Independence came again for both countries in 1991, with the collapse of the USSR.

However, the danger of Russian predation remained a constant feature of their respective national security calculations, culminating in parallel decisions by Riga and Talinn in 2004 to join both the NATO alliance and the European Union. Their concerns were well placed. Russia has repeatedly attempted to stir up trouble (in the form of separatist and anti-establishment sentiments) among the approximately 22 percent of Estonia's 1.3-million-person population who are Russian, as well as the 23 percent of the citizens of Latvia (population 2.8 million) who are as well. It has done so through, among other things, an extensive information warfare campaign, transmitted through Russian-language news channels. As a result, both governments have developed substantial programs designed to combat Russian information warfare.[69] Further, fears of a potential fifth column led Latvia's parliament, the Seimas, to pass a 2022 law banning the use of Russian in all public offices, businesses and venues.[70] The same measure required Russians living in Latvia to apply for permanent residence status and demonstrate a good grasp of the Latvian culture. More recently, in a controversial move, the Seimas also mandated that Russians residing in the country also demonstrate a level of proficiency in the Latvian language.[71]

Estonia may address the problem in another way. The country's Interior Minister, Lauri Laanemets, has signaled that her government is prepared to

69   For an overview of these efforts, see Ilan Berman, *Challenging Moscow's Message: Russian Disinformation and the Western Response* (AFPC Press, 2023).

70   "Latvia: a law passes in Parliament to ban the use of the Russian language," Agenzia Nova, September 24, 2022, https://www.agenzianova.com/en/news/Latvia-passes-a-law-in-parliament-to-ban-the-use-of-the-Russian-language/.

71   Marija Andrejeva, " 'Express Your Loyalty': Russian Speakers In Latvia Face Language Test – Or Deportation," *Radio Free Europe/Radio Liberty*, September 16, 2024, https://www.rferl.org/a/russia-latvia-residents-deportation/33116047.html.

examine the possibility of deporting anyone who chooses to obtain Russian citizenship.[72] Moreover, Laanemets suggested that securing Russian citizenship could in the future be construed as support for terrorism and actions against the Estonian state.[73]

Recently, more serious threats have emanated from Moscow. For instance, a May 2023 social media post by Dmitri Medvedev, Deputy Chairman of Russia's National Security Council, bluntly identified Lithuania, Latvia, and Estonia as "our provinces."[74] In line with this sentiment, in May 2024 Russian officials removed the buoys demarcating the maritime border between Estonia and Russia, thus signaling their country's "intention to challenge such boundaries."[75] These and other threats contributed to the 2024 decision by NATO to post Alliance troops in both Baltic states.

In **Lithuania**, similar fears of Moscow predominate. The country dates its independence to the early 13th century, and by the end of the 14th had built an empire extending from the Baltic Sea to the Black Sea. The Polish-Lithuanian Commonwealth, created in 1569, ruled over most of that territory for 226 years until 1795, when Lithuania, along with Poland, became part of the Russian Empire. It remained so until two years of armed struggle against Germany, the Soviets and newly independent Poland (from 1918 to 1920) led to a second round of independence that lasted until 1940, when the country was jointly occupied by Nazi Germany and the Soviet Union. Thereafter, a victorious USSR brought Lithuania under its sway, where it remained until the 1991 Soviet collapse.

In the post-Soviet era, as Russia gradually regained its geopolitical and economic strength, Lithuania became the target of increasingly hostile actions driven by Russia's neo-imperialist ambitions – primarily via extensive information warfare designed to "increase the will to obey" the

---

72   See, for instance, "Estonia considers deporting individuals who seek to obtain Russian passports," *The New Voice of Ukraine*, December 2, 2023, https://english.nv.ua/nation/estonia-eyes-deportation-for-russian-passport-seekers-50373190.html.

73   Ibid.

74   Joshua Askew, "Ex Russian PM Dmitry Medvedev claims Baltic countries belong to Russia," *Euronews*, May 17, 2023, https://www.euronews.com/2023/05/17/russias-dmitry-medvedev-claims-baltic-countries-belong-to-russia.

75   "Missing Baltic buoys mark out maritime border faultlines," *Financial Times*, May 26, 2024, https://www.ft.com/content/cf2c092d-66b2-4406-9670-48d9448182cc.

Kremlin and "reduce the will to defend" Lithuanian society against Russian encroachment.[76] The potential for destabilization spawned fears among Lithuanian officials that helped drive the country of 2.8 million to become a full member of NATO as well as the European Union in 2004.

Russia's informational onslaught has persisted nonetheless. By 2022, Russia was estimated to have launched roughly 5,000 disinformation attacks against Lithuania. Themes promoted by Russian information operations included the destabilizing regional effects of the war in Ukraine, the dangers of NATO membership, and the ill-treatment of the roughly 5 percent of Lithuania's population that is Russian.[77] In response, Lithuania has developed an intricate counter-disinformation mechanism, involving weekly meetings of relevant government officials, fusion centers and rapid response capabilities in the informational space, armed forces units tasked with observing and countering "hostile" (foreign) influences on society.[78] In this way, successive governments in Vilnius have sought to strengthen the will of their people to resist Russian ideology and imperial messaging.

Russia remains covetous of **Georgia** as well. Tbilisi, for its part, has a long history with imperial encroachment. Over its more than 2,500-year history, the country has dominated many smaller ethnic groups and, in turn, been absorbed into successive empires. Over the years, its masters have included the Mongols, the Arabs, the Greeks, the Persians, the Russians, as well as the Turks. In the context of Russia, Georgia represents a classic case of gradual absorption. Russia annexed parts of Georgia in 1783, 1801,1803, 1804, 1810,1813, 1828, 1833, 1857,1858, and 1864, before complete annexation took place in 1878. During the Russian civil war, Georgia proclaimed independence for three years (1918-1921) before falling under Moscow's sway once more, where it remained until emerging as an independent state following the 1991 collapse of the USSR.

This trajectory was opposed by Moscow. Practically from the start, Russia worked diligently to undermine Georgia's independence. During

---

76 Berman, *Challenging Moscow's Message*, 64.

77 Ibid., 63-65.

78 Ibidem.

fighting in 1992-1993, for instance, an estimated 10,000 lives were lost as Russian and Abkhaz fighters drove Georgians out of Abkhazia, then a northwestern Georgian province.[79] In the aftermath of the fighting, almost all ethnic Georgians, who numbered nearly 400,000 in 1989, left the province. After fighting briefly resumed in 2008, Russia formally recognized the independence of the 250,000-person region. In practice, it is now part of Russia, as is the even smaller (50,000 person) Georgian province of South Ossetia, which also gained Russian support for its independence following Russian-backed fighting in 2008 that completely removed Georgian troops from the region.

Since then, Moscow has focused on installing and maintaining a pro-Russian government in Tbilisi, with considerable success. This policy was best expressed by Andrei Klimov, Deputy Chairman of the Federation Council, the upper house of Russia's parliament, who noted in July 2024 noted that, if asked, Russia would assist the pro-Kremlin "Georgia Dream" to remain in power.[80] Increasingly, Moscow's actions mimic its 19th century policy of gradually absorbing the entirety of the Georgian state.

Simultaneously, Moscow has focused on eroding the sovereignty of **Moldova**. The territory of the present-day nation, a country of 3.4 million, was ruled by the Romans, the Huns, the Ostogoths, the Antes, the Bulgarians, the Magyars, the Pechenegs and the Hungarians before the emergence of the Moldovan Principality in 1349.That independence was crushed by the Ottomans, who ruled the area from 1512 until the early 19th century, when the land was conquered by the Russian Empire. In the aftermath of World War I and the Russian revolution, Moldova briefly proclaimed its independence before uniting with Romania. Then, in 1924, the Soviet Union gained the territory east of the Dnestr, and in 1940 – as an ally of Nazi Germany – occupied much of the land to its west. The 1947 Paris Peace Treaty awarded the remaining parts of today's Moldova to the Soviet Union, which had joined the winning side after being betrayed by its ally

---

79   See, for instance, Greenberg Research, Inc. "Country Report: Georgia/Abkhazia," n.d., https://www.icrc.org/sites/default/files/external/doc/en/assets/files/other/georgia.pdf.

80   "Russian Official Doesn't Rule out Possible Help for GD to Remain in Power," civil.ge, July 22, 2024, https://civil.ge/archives/617050.

Germany. In 1950, under the oversight of Leonid Brezhnev, then the First Secretary of the Central Committee of the Moldovan SSR, the Soviet Union deported 100,000 of its citizens to Romania and imprisoned many others.

Force was again used between November 1990 and June 1992, when Russia's 14th Army, led by General Alexander Lebed, intervened in the Moldovan civil war, ensuring that Moldovan sovereignty over Transdneister was replaced by *de facto* Russian control. That might have turned out to be a prelude for things to come. Had Russia succeeded in its 2022 goal of conquering the southern part of Ukraine, it is highly likely that Transdneister would have been annexed to Russia – something that had been discussed for decades in Moscow.

Nevertheless, such an erosion of Moldovan sovereignty very much remains a strategic goal of the Kremlin. Throughout the entire period of post-Soviet Moldovan independence, Moscow has worked to put pro-Russian politicians into national positions of power, in part by way of destabilizing the Moldovan state. This ongoing pressure, as well as Russia's current war on Ukraine, has revived long-running discussions of a possible union with Romania as a protective measure – something that the country's leadership previously rejected.[81] The about-face is logical, since such a step could confer clear strategic benefits to Chisinau, instantly making Moldova a part of the EU and NATO and thereby ensuring greater prosperity and security.

Meanwhile, **Poland** finds itself in a more preferential position, owing to the country's current political vibrancy, economic prosperity and membership in NATO. Nevertheless, Russia has had historical designs on the Polish state that date back centuries.

The conversion to Christianity of Polish Prince Mieszko I in 966 AD is viewed as the origin of the modern Polish state. Despite contractions and expansions, the territory of Poland and the Polish-Lithuanian commonwealth (1569–1795) remained independent until the third partition of Poland in 1795. Along with the previous two partitions (1772 and 1793), Czarist Russia and, to a lesser degree, Germany and Austria annexed all of

---

81   Jennifer Rankin, "Moldova PM rules out reunification with Romania," *The Guardian*, May 11, 2024, https://www.theguardian.com/world/2018/may/11/moldova-pm-pavel-filip-rules-out-reunification-romania.

Poland. With the defeat of Germany, Russia, and Austria in World War I, a Polish independence movement arose, culminating in Polish Marshall Jozef Pilsudski's 1921 defeat of the Red Army led by Leon Trotsky. That victory secured Polish independence until the joint Soviet-Nazi invasion of 1939. Following the Second World War, the extensive presence of the Soviet military resulted in a nominally independent Poland becoming a satellite state of the USSR. Despite multiple movements for independence within its borders, this state of affairs would persist until Poland's successful January 1990 exit from a crumbling Soviet Union.

But historic fears of predation remained and, worried about yet another attack by a future Russian government, Poland sought to improve the security of its borders by formally joining NATO in 1999. For its part, Russia has not given up its designs on Poland. Thus, in a throwback to past Russian campaigns and occupations, Deputy Security Council chairman Dmitry Medvedev wrote publicly in November 2023 that: "History has more than once delivered a merciless verdict to the presumptuous Poles… their collapse could lead to the death of the Polish statehood in its entirety."[82] This and similar Russian statements are taken very seriously in Poland, where officials are convinced that, if Ukraine is fully occupied by Russia, their country will invariably be next.[83]

Finally, there is **Finland**, where Russia has systematically sought to erode state sovereignty in recent years through an array of asymmetric measures. Moscow's interest is logical, insofar as Finland was once a Russian holding. Imperial Russia's defeat of Sweden in the Finnish War of 1808-1809 ended the latter's six-hundred-year rule of Finnish territory, and thereafter, for a period of 108 years (from 1809 until 1917), Finland was ruled by the Russian Czar. Subsequently, in the aftermath of World War I and Russia's

---

82   "Putin ally warns 'enemy' Poland: you risk losing your statehood,"
      Reuters, November 2, 2023, https://www.reuters.com/world/europe/
      putin-ally-warns-enemy-poland-you-risk-losing-your-statehood-2023-11-02/.

83   See, for instance, Isabel van Brugen, "Poland Issues Grim Prediction for
      Russia if It Attacks," *Newsweek*, April 29, 2024, https://www.newsweek.com/
      poland-radoslaw-sikorski-russia-nato-attack-1895017.

civil war, Finland gained independence in 1917 and has maintained it since in spite of repeated Soviet challenges to its territorial integrity.[84]

With Russia's war on Ukraine, these challenges have begun anew. Since Russia's 2022 invasion of Ukraine, Moscow has launched a series of aggressive actions against Finland. These include repeated violations of Finnish air space, Moscow's withdrawal from a longstanding Finnish-Russian border agreement,[85] and various provocative actions in Finland's Aland Islands, whose nearby sea lanes carry 96 percent of Finland's trade.[86] These maneuvers prompted a strategic rethink in Helsinki, and in 2023, the Nordic nation abandoned its decades-long policy of neutrality and sought membership in NATO in order to bolster its defenses against any potential Russian aggression. Finland was formally admitted to the Alliance the same year.

A Widening Reach

The third strain of Russia's revived imperialism is directed toward acquiring new lands – that is, territories that were never part of either the Russian Empire or the Soviet Union. These include parts of Denmark, Sweden, and Norway. While the Kremlin has officially denied that it harbors designs on these countries, their respective national leaderships are convinced that hostile action by Moscow remains a real possibility, owing to a number of factors.

Denmark, for instance, maintains competing territorial claims with Russia to a broad swathe of the Arctic Ocean seabed (some 800,000 square kilometers, or 308,882 square miles). These competing claims are significant, since the Arctic's continental shelf is believed to hold one quarter of the

---

84   The most notable of these were the Soviet invasions of 1940 and 1944, both of which resulted in Finland ceding territory to the Soviet Union and agreeing to limitations on its sovereignty.

85   Pierre Emmanuel Ngendakumana, "After Putin vowed 'problems,' Russia ends cross-border deal with Finland," *Politico*, January 25, 2024, https://www.politico.eu/article/russia-terminates-cross-border-cooperation-agreement-with-finland/?utm_source=Twitter&utm_medium=social.

86   See, for instance, Anna-Sophie Schneider, "What Happens If Russia Attacks Finland's Aland Islands?" *Der Spiegel*, July 6, 2023, https://www.spiegel.de/international/europe/a-strategic-baltic-archipelago-what-happens-if-russia-attacks-finland-s-aland-islands-a-87f17866-50bf-4b43-b021-23a80939aeeb.

world's undiscovered hydrocarbon reserves.[87] And while international law favors Denmark's claim, political will is operative here – and serious problems will arise if a dominant Russian military presence is used to enforce the Kremlin's claims.

Moscow's arguments are serious, and detailed. As President Putin himself laid out in 2014, at a meeting of the country's Security Council:

> For dozens of years, systematically, Russia has been strengthening, enhancing its presence, its positions in the Arctic… Primarily this is done by restoring the number of airfields beyond the Arctic Circle and the military base on the New Siberian Islands. We are optimizing the army groups and naval forces in the area.[88]

Russian military policy has tracked with this imperative. As Navy Admiral Nikolai Yevmenov has explained, "there is need for a full-scale expansion into the continental shelf beyond the borders of the 200-mile economic zone… The development of our military component in the Arctic is a forced measure to ward off threat against Russia and stem aggressive actions by other countries."[89] Since 2022, Danish airspace and territorial waters have also repeatedly been breached by Russia, escalating tensions in the region and demonstrating to Denmark that it can do nothing if Russia chooses to enforce its claims by military means.

Russia and **Sweden**, meanwhile, have a long history of military conflict. The two countries have fought 12 wars since the 15th century, the last of them in 1809. In recent years, Stockholm has worried openly about Russian designs on Sweden's largest island, Gotland (which is about the size of the U.S. state of Rhode Island). During its 1808 war with Sweden, Russia had briefly occupied Gotland. Since then, the island has been Swedish terri-

---

87   "The Great Arctic Oil Rush," *New York Times*, August 12, 2007, https://www.nytimes.com/2007/08/12/opinion/12iht-edarctic.1.7088185.html.

88   Office of the President of Russia, "Meeting of the Security Council on state policy in the Arctic," April 22, 2014, http://en.kremlin.ru/events/president/news/20845.

89   As cited in "Russia Insists on an Expanded Boundary in the Arctic Ocean," *The Maritime Executive*, December 10, 2023, https://maritime-executive.com/article/russia-insists-on-an-expanded-boundary-in-the-arctic-ocean.

tory – albeit one that was armed against possible Soviet aggression during the decades of the Cold War. Sweden withdrew forces from the island in 2005, only to replace them following Russia's 2014 invasion of Ukraine, which forced Stockholm to take seriously Moscow's statements desiring dominion over the island.

So, the situation remains. Today, officials in Stockholm are convinced Russia maintains active designs over the territory. "I'm sure that Putin even has both eyes on Gotland," Gen. Micael Byden, Supreme Commander of Sweden's armed forces, has said. "Putin's goal is to gain control of the Baltic Sea."[90] This view has no doubt been reinforced by the Russian military's announcement of plans to expand Russia's territorial waters in the Baltic Sea,[91] as well as Russia's repeated violation of Sweden's air and maritime defense zones. Sweden's worries over Russian intentions led to its decision to formally join the NATO alliance in 2023.

Norway, too, holds territory that the Kremlin covets, in the form of Spitsbergen, the biggest island in the Svalbard archipelago. In 1925, 14 countries ratified a treaty recognizing Norway's sovereignty over the area. In 1935, the Soviet Union signed the treaty, and in 1947 the Storting, Norway's legislature, recognized that the USSR had special economic interests on the island. Subsequently, however, Soviet claims expanded, causing friction with Norway's maritime commercial activities.[92] These claims continued into the post-Cold War era, and in 2017 the Russian newspaper *Kommersant* wrote that Spitsbergen could become the site of a future Norway-Russian conflict.[93] In light of this eventuality, Oslo has worked to strengthen its sovereignty over the island with ecological and other restrictions – restrictions that are seen as unacceptable by Russia. Moscow's offers to dis-

---

90   Liv Martin, "Putin has 'both eyes' on Gotland, wans Sweden's army chief," *Politico*, May 22, 2024, https://www.politico.eu/article/russia-putin-eyes-sweden-gotland-baltic-sea-army-chief/.

91   Sebastian Seibt, "Russia moves to extend its maritime borders, angering Baltic Sea nations," *France 24*, May 23, 2024, https://www.france24.com/en/europe/20240523-russia-moves-extend-maritime-borders-angering-baltic-sea-nations.

92   See, for instance, Andreas Osthagen, "Svalbard and Geopolitics: A Need for Clarity," The Arctic Institute, June 25, 2024, https://www.thearcticinstitute.org/svalbard-geopolitics-need-clarity/.

93   Thomas Nilsen, "Kommersant: Russia lists Norway's Svalbard policy as potential risk of war," *The Barents Observer*, October 4, 2017, https://www.thebarentsobserver.com/security/kommersant-russia-lists-norways-svalbard-policy-as-potential-risk-of-war/155149.

cuss the situation, however, have been rejected by Norway, which views the Russian complaints as an assault on its sovereignty.

An Ideology of Empire

Over the centuries, Russia's deep-seated imperial impulses have been articulated in countless ways. In recent decades, however, they have crystallized into a cohesive ideology of "Eurasianism" that explains, underpins and justifies the country's persistent territorial and geopolitical yearnings.

Eurasianism's early roots and evolution have been extensively documented by scholars such as Marlene Laruelle and Charles Clover.[94] As these analysts lay out, the origins of the philosophy can be traced back to the early 20th century, when thinkers like Count Nikolai Trubetskoi (1890-1938) articulated a philosophy of overriding cultural and political struggle between the West and a distinct Russia-led "Eurasian" subcontinent. These ideas were subsequently carried forward during the Soviet era by public intellectuals like Lev Gumilev (1912-1992), a historian and ethnologist whose theories about identity and nativism became broadly popular (including among Russian elites).[95]

Today, the most conspicuous proponent of the doctrine is unquestionably Alexander Dugin. Over the past three decades, the controversial KGB archivist-turned-ideologue has carved out a prominent place for himself on the Russian political scene as a champion of renewed imperialism on the part of the Kremlin. His vision is most clearly articulated in his 1997 work *Osnovi Geopolitiki: Geopolitichiskoye Budushiye Rossiyi* (*The Foundations of Geopolitics: The Geopolitical Future of Russia*), in which he posits a vision of overriding competition with the West, Russian imperial destiny, and the need for anti-Western partnership among likeminded states. Thus, "the strategic interests of the Russian people must be oriented in an anti-Western fashion (deriving from the imperative to preserve the identity of Russia's civ-

---

94   Marlene Laruelle, *Russian Eurasianism: An Ideology of Empire* (Johns Hopkins University Press, 2008); Charles Clover, *Black Wind, White Snow: Russia's New Nationalism* (Yale University Press, 2022).
95   "Prominent Russians: Lev Gumilev," *RT*, n.d., https://russiapedia.rt.com/prominent-russians/science-and-technology/lev-gumilev/.

ilization)," Dugin has written.[96] He likewise argues that Russia "cannot exist outside of its essence as an empire, by its geographical situation, historical path and fate of the state."[97]

In the late 1990s and early 2000s, these concepts fueled the rise of a fledgling Eurasianist political movement in Moscow,[98] until the terrorist attacks of September 11, 2001 and the subsequent U.S.-led "global war on terror" led the Kremlin to acquiesce to a Western presence along Russia's periphery. This accommodation proved to be short-lived, however, and within just a few years Russia had resumed its efforts to exert dominance and hegemony over the "post-Soviet space." Eurasianism's resurgence broadly paralleled this reversion to type, and – since Vladimir Putin's triumphant return to the Russian presidency in 2012, following constitutional changes which have made possible a more-or-less permanent reign – the doctrine has steadily gained ground. Thus, Dugin's formulation of the Slavic parts of Ukraine as "Novorossiya" (New Russia) were embraced by the Kremlin and used in official propaganda in support of Russia's invasion and annexation of Crimea in 2014.[99] Today, Dugin is an ardent supporter of Putin's new war of choice against Kyiv, even advocating the use of extreme measures in order for Russia to persevere in what he depicts as a proxy battle in a larger existential conflict with the West.[100]

The extent of Dugin's influence is the subject of considerable debate. To some, Dugin is effectively "Putin's Brain," the mastermind behind Russia's international maneuvers and something resembling a Rosetta Stone for understanding what makes the Russian strongman tick.[101] Others, however, have dismissed Dugin's relevance, styling him as merely a marginal figure.

---

96 Alexandr Dugin, *Osnovi Geopolitiki: Geopoliticheskoyo Budushiye Rossii* (Moscow: Arctogia Centr, 1999), 190. (author's trans.)

97 As cited in Charles Clover, "Will the Russian Bear Roar Again?" *Financial Times*, December 2, 2000.

98 Victor Yasmann, "Rise of the Eurasians," *RFE/RL Security Watch* 2, no. 17, April 30, 2001.

99 Tara Isabella Burton, "The far-right mystical writer who's helped shape Putin's view of Russia," *Washington Post*, May 12, 2022, https://www.washingtonpost.com/outlook/2022/05/12/dugin-russia-ukraine-putin/.

100 See, for instance, Edward Stawiarski, "Alexandr Dugin: 'I see no reason why we should not use nuclear weapons,'" *The Spectator* (UK), January 6, 2024, https://www.spectator.co.uk/article/i-see-no-reason-why-we-should-not-use-nuclear-weapons-an-interview-with-russian-philosopher-aleksandr-dugin/.

101 See, for instance, Ayesha Rascoe, "Russian intellectual Aleksandr Dugin is also commonly known as 'Putin's brain,'" *NPR*, March 27, 2022, https://www.npr.org/2022/03/27/1089047787/russian-intellectual-aleksandr-dugin-is-also-commonly-known-as-putins-brain.

What is unquestionable, however, is that the ideas he has championed about Russia's imperial imperative are shared by a broad swathe of the country's political elites and decisionmakers.

Their ranks include individuals like Vladislav Surkov, a key Kremlin advisor and Putin confidante, who has echoed the idea that Russia's "innate status" is one of a great power, with a global role assigned "by world history."[102] Others, like former Defense Minister Sergei Shoigu and current Foreign Minister Sergei Lavrov, are on record espousing similar views. And there is ample evidence that Russian president Vladimir Putin himself believes much the same thing. As numerous scholars have noted, Putin has persistently articulated the notion of Russian greatness in his public addresses and proclamations, and has made a revitalization of the concept of *Derzhavnost* – the recreation of great power status – a top priority from his first days in office.[103]

This vision has distinct imperial overtones. While some in the West have depicted Russia's recent maneuvers as simply an attempt to recreate the Soviet Union,[104] this is entirely too modest a formulation. Putin's ambitions are, in actuality, far broader, and driven by a sense of imperial destiny that has led Moscow to repeatedly attempt to revise the post-Cold War order in its favor, and to the profound detriment of the West.

---

102 Vladislav Surkov, "Долгое государство Путина [The long government of Putin]," *Nezavisimaya Gazeta*, February 11, 2019, https://www.ng.ru/ideas/2019-02-11/5_7503_surkov.html?print=Y.

103 See, for instance, Fiona Hill and Clifford Gaddy, *Mr. Putin: Operative of the Kremlin* (Brookings Institution Press, 2013), 38-39, 238.

104 Michael R. Pompeo, "Putin wants to bring back the Soviet Union. We must not allow that to happen," *Fox News*, February 24, 2022, https://www.foxnews.com/opinion/bidens-approach-ukraine-russia-wrong-start-mike-pompeo.

Iran: An Islamist Impulse for Expansion

Although the contemporary literature on Iran focuses overwhelmingly on the Ayatollah Ruhollah Khomeini's Islamic Revolution of 1979, and on the radical clerical regime that has ruled the country since, Iran can only be fully understood in the context of its imperial past. Before to the Islamic Revolution, Iran was formally known as the "Empire of Iran" - reflecting the succession of empires that had preceded it, from the Achaemenids (500-330 BC) to the Qajars (1796-1925). As these successive Persian empires waxed and waned, they brought diverse areas of the world under their control.

In antiquity, for instance, the areas controlled by the Achaemenids encompassed all of modern-day Afghanistan and Pakistan, as well as a significant portion of contemporary Central Asia. The Sassanid Empire (224-651 AD) subsequently extended its reach westward over the entirety of Turkey and into the Balkans. And at the height of its power in the late 1600s, the Safavid Dynasty (1502-1736) covered a swath of territory stretching from central Afghanistan to southeastern Turkey and northward to encompass nearly the entirety of today's North Caucasus republics of Georgia, Armenia and Azerbaijan.

This geographic sweep brought millions of people and dozens of distinct ethnic groups under the sway of Persia, creating a complex patchwork of ethnicities and cultures that helped to shape national politics within Iran. It also left indelible traces on many former imperial holdings. Thus, the Shi'a community of contemporary India – which, at over 45 million, represents the largest Shi'a Diaspora globally[105] – is an artifact of the Achaemenid invasion of northwestern India in 550BC, and the Emperor Cyrus' subsequent successful campaign to unite local Indian tribes under Persian control. Likewise, the area that is modern-day Tajikistan was part of the Achaemenid Empire in antiquity, and again between 819-999 CE, before being subsumed by the Mongols and Russians. Persian imperial control, in turn, shaped the development of the country's language, which in its contemporary form is Farsi written in a Cyrillic alphabet.[106]

Unquestionably, though, the 1979 Islamic Revolution was a seminal political and ideological event in Iran's evolution. It ended more than a millennium of imperial continuity, transforming the country from a monarchy into a radical religious theocracy. The religious revolt spearheaded by Khomeini was groundbreaking, insofar as it fundamentally redefined the prevailing interpretation of Shi'a Islam, which over the centuries had become quietist and largely divorced from regional politics, into one of political activism and engagement.[107] The vision articulated by Khomeini, outlined in detail in his manifesto *Islamic Government*, was one of religious-based imperialism – championing the establishment of radical religious-based rule in Iran and its subsequent expansion beyond the borders of a transformed Iran.[108] In keeping with this dictum, the preamble of the Islamic Republic's first post-1979 constitution announced that the country's armed forces "will be responsible not only for guarding and preserving the frontiers of the country, but also for fulfilling the ideological mission of jihad in God's way; that is, extending the sovereignty of God's law throughout the world."[109]

Over the decades, Iran has sought to fulfill this imperative through two primary ways: 1) the creation of an extensive network of proxy organizations and radical groups, and 2) pervasive influence over the politics (and in some cases strategic affairs) of former imperial holdings. The particulars

105   "The Shias of India," Ahlulbayt, October 4, 2016, https://www.youtube.com/watch?v=mx19SV3kmis.
106   https://translateswift.com/languages/tajik/.
107   See generally Vali Nasr, *The Shia Revival: How Conflicts Within Islam Will Shape the Future* (WW Norton & Co., 2007).
108   Ayatollah Ruhollah Khomeini (Joint Publication Research Service, trans.), *Islamic Government* (Manor Books, 1979).
109   "Preamble," Constitution of Iran, October 24, 1979, https://www.servat.unibe.ch/icl/ir00000_.html.

have varied; in parts of its old empire, such as Lebanon and Yemen, the Islamic Republic currently exerts influence via proxy groups such as Hezbollah or through manipulation of the prevailing political system (for example, via its support of Yemen's Houthi rebels). In others (like Syria until the fall of Bashar al-Assad's regime in December 2024), it wields more direct military control.

Whatever the method employed by Tehran, however, the results have been marked. A decade ago, Iranian officials were already boasting that their government had succeeded in capturing and controlling four separate Arab capitals in the Middle East: Damascus, Syria; Baghdad, Iraq; Beirut, Lebanon; and Sana'a, Yemen.[110] Since then, regional instability and the weakness of local governance has allowed Tehran to expand its ambit still further, while feckless U.S. policy has provided the Iranian regime the resources to do so.

So significant has the threat of further Iranian expansion by force been that, in recent years, it spurred a grand realignment in the region, with Israel and its traditional Sunni state adversaries drawing closer in response to what, for many, represents an existential threat to their sovereignty and territorial integrity. The result was the signing, in 2020, of the Abraham Accords between Israel and Bahrain, the United Emirates and Sudan, followed closely thereafter by Israel's normalization with Morocco. While the tragic events of October 7, 2023, and Israel's ensuing war against Hamas in the Gaza Strip have temporarily derailed this process, there is a broad consensus that it will be revived again in due course.[111] That consensus is underpinned not only by the internal logic of the Accords themselves, but also by the shared threat of an expansionist and increasingly aggressive Islamic Republic.

Undergirding Iran's persistent efforts to expand its political and ideological ambit is a conviction on the part of the country's clerical elites that their regime represents, in the words of scholar Graham Fuller, "the

---

110   Mamoon Alabbasi, "Iran Continues to Boast of its Regional Reach," *Middle East Eye,* March 10, 2015, https://www.middleeasteye.net/news/iran-continues-boast-its-regional-reach.

111   Neville Teller, "The Abraham Accords will probably survive – opinion," *Jerusalem Post,* April 1, 2024, https://www.jpost.com/opinion/article-794600.

center of the universe" – the geopolitical fulcrum of the Middle East around which the region should naturally revolve.[112] For nearly half-a-century, this deeply-held conviction has propelled the regime into persistent conflict with countries along its periphery.

Dominating Iraq

Today, Iran wields extensive influence over Iraqi politics and society. Following the 2003 ouster of Iraqi strongman Saddam Hussein by the U.S.-led Coalition, Iran intruded into the country's politics, eventually assuming commanding influence through a mix of political manipulation, sectarian dynamics, and paramilitary organizations.[113] The partnership between Baghdad and Tehran, however, is unequal, with the latter playing the role of senior partner. It also contains a number of notable flashpoints.

Some are territorial, such as the 120-mile Shatt al-Arab river. Between 1936 and 1975, the two countries maintained competing claims to the area, which represents a critical passageway for the export of oil from the Middle East. The competition stretched back centuries, to Persian-Ottoman disputes which culminated in the signing of the 1639 Treaty of Zuhab demarcating the boundary between Persia and what was then Mesopotamia. With the emergence of modern Iraq in 1937, that understanding was modernized in a formal treaty between Baghdad and Tehran. But Iraq's transformation into a Ba'athist state in 1968 led to a deterioration of relations with Iran that included an abrogation of the Shatt al-Arab understanding and tensions along the waterway – a situation that would persist until the 1975 Algiers agreement. The area subsequently became a flashpoint that helped trigger the Iran-Iraq War, culminating in a return to the Algiers agreement. Nevertheless, the waterway has remained troublesome, and on at least two occasions during the Second Gulf War (in 2004 and then again in 2007), Iranian seizure of British naval assets and personnel threatened to transform

---

112   See Graham E. Fuller, *The Center of the Universe: The Geopolitics of Iran* (Santa Monica: RAND, 1991).

113   See, for instance, Muhanad Seloom, "From Rivals to Allies: Iran's Evolving Role in Iraq's Geopolitics," Middle East Council on Global Affairs, April 2024, https://mecouncil.org/publication_chapters/from-rivals-to-allies-irans-evolving-role-in-iraqs-geopolitics/

it into a global flashpoint. Today, disputes over the Shatt al-Arab persist, and despite their present, close political relations, Tehran and Baghdad continue to contest its land, sea and coastal borders.[114]

Other issues are ideological in nature. Iraq is the home nation of the Grand Ayatollah Ali al-Sistani, Shi'a Islam's most senior and venerated cleric. Notably, Sistani both practices and preaches an austere, quietist version of the faith – one that is at fundamental odds with the political, activist strain embodied in the Islamic Republic's ruling doctrine of *velayat e-faqih* (Guardianship of the Jurist). This, coupled with the comparative lack of seniority of Iran's current Supreme Leader, Ali Khamenei (who became the consensus candidate upon Khomeini's death in 1979 despite his comparatively junior religious status[115]) has led to Sistani being seen by Iran's leadership as a serious threat to their legitimacy. Accordingly, the cleric (now aged 95) has been held under house arrest by forces loyal to the Islamic Republic since Iran's clandestine penetration into the country in the wake of 2003's Operation Iraqi Freedom.[116] As the Islamic Republic today approaches a succession crisis, continued erosion of Iraqi sovereignty – and, by extension, the authority and independence of its Shi'a community – represents an important priority.

Transforming Syria

Iran's involvement in what is today Syria is both intimate and historic. During his reign in the 6th century BC, Persian emperor Cyrus took control of Syrian territory as he expanded his empire. That control would last until the territory was wrested from Persian hands by Alexander the Great some 200 years later. Thereafter, Syria again came under the sway of the Persians,

---

114   "Iraq Says Still At Odds With Iran Over Border," *Radio Free Europe/Radio Liberty*, March 9, 2009, https://www.rferl.org/a/Iraq_Says_Still_At_Odds_With_Iran_Over_Border/1506725.html.

115   See generally Mehdi Khalaji, *The Regent of Allah: Ali Khamenei's Political Evolution in Iran* (Rowman & Littlefield, 2023).

116   Sajad Jiyad, "Iran and Iraq Are Competing Over Leadership of Shiite Islam After Sistani," *New Lines Magazine*, July 3, 2024, https://newlinesmag.com/argument/iran-and-iraq-are-competing-over-leadership-of-shiite-islam-after-sistani/.

this time in the form of the Sasanian empire, in the 7th century AD, before being subsumed by Ottoman control early in the 16th Century.

Ottoman rule lasted for four centuries, during which time Syria was governed from Constantinople in the form of a series of administrative provinces. By the early 20th century, Arab nationalist sentiment started to emerge among Syria's intelligentsia, culminating in the 1916 Arab Revolt. That uprising was supported by Britain and weakened Ottoman control over Syria. In the aftermath of the First World War, Ottoman control collapsed entirely and Syria fell to French control, which would last until the upheaval of World War II paved the way for Damascus to declare independence.

Syria established formal diplomatic relations with Iran upon its independence in 1946. In the decades that followed, the two countries maintained favorable relations, punctuated by successive cooperation agreements and extensive diplomatic contacts. Over time, however, warming ties between Iran and neighboring Iraq shouldered Syria aside, as a result of which Syrian President Hafez al-Assad began a flirtation with Iranian anti-Shah dissidents. Thus, when Khomeini's revolution took place in 1979, the stage was set for a warming of ties between Tehran and Damascus.

In the years that followed, Iran's clerical regime succeeded in erecting a robust strategic partnership that provided Tehran with extensive political and economic leverage over Damascus. Iran's rulers have used this leverage to great effect – as a reliable conduit for their support to Lebanon's Hezbollah militia, as a more proximate adversary to preoccupy Israel, and as an integral part of the "axis of resistance" against America and the Jewish state.[117]

The start of the Syrian Civil War in March 2011 provided the Iranian regime a further opening to consolidate its control over Damascus. In the years that followed, the Islamic Republic provided the embattled Assad regime with manpower, material and financing as part of an extensive effort to keep Assad in power. At the same time, the Islamic Republic also worked

---

117   See, for instance, Hamidreza Azizi and Julien Barnes-Dacey, "Beyond Proxies: Iran's Deeper Strategy in Syria and Lebanon," European Council on Foreign Relations *Policy Brief,* June 5, 2024, https://ecfr.eu/publication/beyond-proxies-irans-deeper-strategy-in-syria-and-lebanon/.

diligently to create the requisite conditions to retain its Syrian presence should the Syrian regime fall.[118]

This involved, among other things, reconfiguring – to the extent possible – the very demographics of the Syrian state itself. Thus, the years after Iran's entry into the civil war saw it attempt to effectuate a shift in the composition of Syria's population via the importation of thousands of Shi'ites into the country.[119] The results were pronounced. In pre-war Syria, the country's population of 21 million was 59 percent Sunni, 11 percent Alawite and just 4 percent Shi'ite. By 2022, the Shi'ite percentage of the population had grown to 10 percent, in the process expanding options for Iran in its recruitment and mobilization of sympathetic forces.[120]

It remains to be seen, however, whether this expanded footprint is sustainable. In early December of 2024, Syrian opposition forces, spearheaded by one-time al-Qaeda affiliate Hayat Tahrir al-Sham, launched a redoubled offensive against the Assad regime. The offensive caught government forces by surprise, and Syrian government control crumbled in city after city, culminating in Assad's flight from power. Assad's ouster could rebound to Iran's profound detriment as well. Just days after the fall of his regime, the Iranian government was already reporting the return of thousands of Iranians from Syrian territory amid a larger Iranian retrenchment and fears of Sunni Islamism.[121] Other signs (economic, political and otherwise) also point to the fact that Tehran faces a new, increasingly inhospitable environment in post-Assad Syria.

Nevertheless, observers note, the Islamic Republic still retains options by which to preserve its strategic foothold in Syria. These range from the pursuit of a "sectarian strategy" of strengthened connections to the country's Shi'a and Alawite communities in order to erect a pro-Iranian constituency

118   Will Fulton, Joseph Holliday, and Sam Wyer, *Iranian Strategy in Syria* (Institute for the Study of War, May 2013), https://www.understandingwar.org/sites/default/files/IranianStrategyinSyria-1MAY.pdf.

119   Martin Chulov, "Iran repopulates Syria with Shia Muslims to help tighten regime's control," *Guardian*, January 13, 2017, https://www.theguardian.com/world/2017/jan/13/ irans-syria-project-pushing-population-shifts-to-increase-influence.

120   "Syria's new demographics create recruitment options for Iran, Hezbollah," jns.org, April 7, 2022, https://www.jns.org/syrias-new-demographics-create-recruitment-options-for-iran-hezbollah/.

121   "Tehran says 4,000 Iranians returned from Syria since al-Assad's fall," *Al-Arabiya English*, December 10, 2024, https://english.alarabiya.net/News/middle-east/2024/12/10/ tehran-says-4-000-iranians-returned-from-syria-since-al-assad-s-fall.

within those cohorts, to the fomentation of an insurgency against the new, Sunni-led political order.[122]

The Emirates: Staking a Claim

The United Arab Emirates and Iran have a complex relationship, punctuated by wary diplomatic contacts and deep political divisions. The proximity of the two countries (separated only by the 21-mile-wide Hormuz Strait) has created significant economic links and cultural interplay. These links have been further strengthened by a significant community of Iranians residing in the UAE, particularly in the Emirate of Dubai – a natural byproduct of centuries of commerce between Gulf Arab tribes and imperial Iran.[123] Nevertheless, the two countries harbor significant territorial disputes, centering on three islands in the Persian Gulf. These islands – Abu Musa and the Greater and Lesser Tunbs – have been points of contention for centuries.

Abu Musa, located near the Strait of Hormuz, occupies a strategic location that has made it a significant prize for competing regional powers. Iran traces its claim to it back to antiquity, with successive empires incorporating the island into their respective maritime domains. But various Arab tribes also staked a claim, laying the foundation for today's dispute. With the expansion of British control over the area in the 1900s, the *status quo* shifted, with London recognizing the validity of Gulf claims rather than Iranian ones. Nevertheless, frictions persisted, with Iran's ruling Qajar dynasty periodically asserting ownership of the island in defiance of the Arabs (and the British). That state of affairs lasted until Britain's retraction from the region in the late 1960s. The 1971 establishment of the UAE was followed soon after by a Memorandum of Understanding between Sharjah and Pahlavi-era Iran that created a framework for administrative control of the island. Nevertheless, since the early 1990s, Iran has attempted to alter

---

122   See Diana Rahima, "Syria's Collapse: Strategic Implications for Iran," AFPC *Iran Strategy Brief* no. 15, May 2025, https://www.afpc.org/publications/policy-papers/syrias-collapse-strategic-implications-for-iran.

123   As of 2025, Iranians made up some 540,000, or nearly 5 percent, of the UAE's total population of 11.35 million. See https://www.globalmediainsight.com/blog/uae-population-statistics/.

this balance, including through a military build-up on the island itself[124] and via military exercises in and around its waters.[125]

Like Abu Musa, the **Greater and Lesser Tunbs** have strategic significance, due to their proximity to the Strait of Hormuz and maritime commerce in the Persian Gulf. Here, too, Iran traces its claim to control of the islands during successive empires in antiquity. British expansion into the region likewise shifted control of the Greater and Lesser Tunbs from imperial Iran to the so-called Trucial States (the precursors of the modern-day Emirates) in the 19th Century. These territories, together with Abu Musa, became part of the British protectorate, which persisted despite periodic Iranian attempts to reclaim sovereignty. On the eve of the UAE's independence in 1971, Iran landed military forces on the islands in an attempt to again wrest their control from the incipient Gulf state.[126] This time, Tehran was successful, and an Iranian military and administrative presence on the islands persists. So, too, does a diplomatic stalemate, under which the Emirates reiterate the historic claim of Ras al-Khaimah to the islands, which are now controlled by Tehran. The islands have occasionally served as a flashpoint in contemporary relations, with Iranians restricting Emirati access to them on "national security" grounds.

It is difficult to divorce these territorial disputes from the larger geopolitical tensions between Iran and the UAE. In recent years, bilateral relations have been badly frayed by the UAE's westward drift and its deepening partnership with the United States. Significant, too, has been the Emirates' leading role in the "Abraham Accords" normalization process with Israel – a process which the Islamic Republic has opposed vehemently. As a result of Abu Dhabi's willingness to normalize its relations with Israel, Iran's Supreme Leader Ali Khamenei has accused the country of "betraying" the

---

124   See, for instance, Faramarz Kuhpayeh, "Hybrid message from Bu Musa," *Tehran Times*, August 4, 2023, https://www.tehrantimes.com/news/487540/Hybrid-message-from-Bu-Musa.

125   "Iran's Revolutionary Guards Runs Drill on Disputed Islands in Persian Gulf," Associated Press, August 2, 2023, https://www.voanews.com/a/iran-s-revolutionary-guard-runs-drill-on-disputed-islands-in-persian-gulf/7209101.html.

126   For a comprehensive overview of the dispute over Abu Musa and the Tunbs islands, see Central Intelligence Agency, "Iran: The Persian Gulf Islands Dispute," Research Paper, May 1980, https://www.cia.gov/readingroom/docs/CIA-RDP08C01297R000500120001-5.pdf.

Muslim World.[127] Should the Iranian regime decide to act on this animus, there is little doubt that its most likely target will be the islands that it claims in defiance of the UAE.

Bringing Back Bahrain

Iran maintains long-standing imperial designs over the Kingdom of Bahrain as well. The country drifted into the Persian orbit in 1602, when the Safavid empire expelled the Portuguese from its territory (which they had ruled for close to 100 years) and established dominion over it. Iran would control Bahrain for more than 350 years thereafter, with the country becoming an integral part of successive Persian empires and assuming the status of imperial Iran's "14th province."

Bahrain's independence was officially recognized by the Iranian parliament in May of 1970, pursuant to which Iran formally renounced its claims to the country. That *status quo* persisted until the Islamic Revolution of 1979 ousted Shah Reza Pahlavi from power in favor of an Islamist theocracy. Thereafter, though the new Iranian regime continued to formally recognize Bahraini independence, its imperial yearnings – as well as the generally strained state of political ties between Tehran and Manama – prompted it to periodically try to subvert Bahrain's sovereignty.

In the years immediately following the 1979 Revolution, Bahraini officials accused Iran of playing a role in seeking to foment a Shi'a revolution in the country.[128] Relations between the two countries receded to a low ebb, but Tehran has continued to covet the majority-Shi'a nation, which it views as having been unjustly ripped from its territory. Thus, a 2007 editorial in the quasi-official *Kayhan* newspaper, known to be close to the office of the country's Supreme Leader, fanned regional worries when it detailed: "Today, the main demand of the people of Bahrain is return of this province, which was severed from Iran, back to its original and maternal

---

127 "Iran's Khamenei says normalising Israel ties is a losing bet – state media," Reuters, October 3, 2023, https://www.reuters.com/world/middle-east/irans-khamenei-says-normalising-ties-with-israel-is-betting-losing-horse-state-2023-10-03/.

128 Steven Wright, "Iran's Relations with Bahrain," in G. Baghat, A. Ehteshami and N. Quilliam, eds., *Security and Bilateral Issues Between Iran and its Arab Neighbours* (London: Palgrave Macmillan, 2017).

land, meaning Islamic Iran. This, obviously, is the incontrovertible right of Iran and the right of the people of the severed province, which must and cannot be ignored."[129] During the ensuing "Arab Spring," Tehran threw its weight behind the country's Shi'a minority in its efforts to unseat the ruling al-Khalifa family.[130]

While Tehran has not yet acted on the impulse, this and other statements have made clear that reacquisition of the "14th province" remains very much on the minds of hardliners in Tehran. [131] These impulses, moreover, have been aggravated by Manama's larger, pro-Western foreign policy direction. Since the 1970s, Bahrain has served as the forward operating base for America's maritime presence in the region, and in this capacity played a pivotal role both in Operation Enduring Freedom, America's post-September 11th campaign against al-Qaeda and the Taliban in Afghanistan, as well as the subsequent Operation Iraqi Freedom that toppled the regime of Iraqi dictator Saddam Hussein. Even more of an irritant, however, has been Bahrain's participation in the "Abraham Accords." In September of 2020, Bahrain joined the UAE and Sudan in normalizing relations with the State of Israel, a decision that drew furious condemnation from Tehran.[132]

For their part, Bahraini officials have attempted to strike some sort of *modus vivendi* with Tehran.[133] In the summer of 2024, the two countries agreed to launch negotiations aimed at restoring regular diplomatic contacts, which had been officially severed since 2016.[134] Despite this progress, however, fears of potential Iranian predation continue to run deep in Manama. These worries have been fanned by Iran's persistent attempts to

---

129   Ali Alfoneh, "Bahrain Reduced to Province of Iran on President Raisi's Instagram," Arab Gulf States Institute in Washington, July 8, 2022, https://agsiw.org/bahrain-reduced-to-province-of-iran-on-president-raisis-instagram/.

130   Semira N. Nikou, "Iran Warns Gulf on Bahrain," PBS *Tehran Bureau*, March 25, 2011, https://www.pbs.org/wgbh/pages/frontline/tehranbureau/2011/03/iran-warns-gulf-on-bahrain.html.

131   See, for instance, "Iran supreme leader: People's will prevail in Bahrain after protests," Reuters, July 31, 2019, https://www.reuters.com/article/world/iran-supreme-leader-peoples-will-prevail-in-bahrain-after-protests-idUSKCN1UQ1M3/.

132   "Iran's Khamenei says normalising Israel ties is a losing bet – state media."

133   William Roebuck, "Bahrain and Iran Aim to Restore Ties," Arab Gulf States Institute in Washington, July 2, 2024, https://agsiw.org/bahrain-and-iran-aim-to-restore-ties/.

134   "Iran, Bahrain agree to discuss restoring ties in latest Gulf-Tehran thaw," Agence France-Presse, June 24, 2024, https://www.timesofisrael.com/iran-bahrain-agree-to-discuss-restoring-ties-in-latest-gulf-tehran-thaw/.

subvert the sovereignty of regional states through political manipulation as well as the activities of its assorted proxy groups.

Qatar: Both Ally and Captive

Iran's relationship with Qatar reflects a different calculus. What is modern-day Qatar became part of Persian imperial territory comparatively later, in the third century AD, with the expansion of the Sasanian empire. Thereafter, Qatar became an important commercial hub for the Persians, granting it a degree of autonomy over the centuries.

In the modern era, Doha has been seen as consistently close to Tehran in both political and economic terms. Iran was among the first regional nations to recognize the new Qatari state in 1971, establishing formal diplomatic relations the following year. Nevertheless, it was not until more recently that the two nations truly became allies. In the 1980s, relations between Doha and Iran were strained on account of Qatar's membership in the Gulf Cooperation Council and the bloc's backing of Saddam Hussein's Iraq during the 1980-1988 Iran-Iraq War. In the 1990s and 2000s, relations between the two improved, and the smaller, more vulnerable Qatar began to rely more and more heavily upon the Iranian regime's patronage to navigate regional and global affairs.

Doha's dependence increased dramatically in 2017, with the outbreak of a diplomatic crisis with assorted Gulf states, who sought to coerce Qatar into changing a number of its policies through an economic and territorial blockade. Notably, among the changes sought was a rollback of the warm political ties between Qatar and Iran, who the rest of the Gulf viewed as a strategic threat and predatory actor. Qatar successfully weathered the blockade, in no small measure thanks to Iran, which provided vital support by opening its airspace and maritime lanes, thereby allowing Qatar to maintain international commerce and preserve its contacts with the international community.

Thereafter, relations between the two blossomed, evidenced by stepped-up diplomatic engagement, new arrangements on issues such as trade and energy, and plans for an array of new joint projects.[135] At the center of these stepped-up relations is the massive South Pars natural gas field in the Strait of Hormuz. Two-thirds of the field lies in Qatari waters, presumably providing Doha with controlling interest over its deposits. However, the Iranian regime has signaled otherwise, and in the past has warned that it would "pursue its interests" over these deposits.[136] So far it has not done so, giving Qatar free rein to exploit the field's energy wealth. Nevertheless, Qatari officials remain deeply apprehensive that this state of affairs could change dramatically in the future.

This situation has helped render Qatar a geopolitical and geoeconomic captive of the Islamic Republic. The current economic plan of Qatar's ruling al-Thani family centers on exploiting its leading global role in the world liquified natural gas (LNG) market. Doha's current development plans envision a near-doubling of the country's annual production of 77 million cubic meters of LNG over the next several years, as well as massive investments in expanded liquification capabilities and infrastructure.[137] This focus is predicated on anticipated future demand for energy driven in part by growing global data and computing requirements, which in the next decade are projected to account for between eight and ten percent of energy consumption on the planet.

This strategy, however, could become imperiled should Iran more aggressively assert its claims to regional resources. For instance, officials in Doha are convinced that Iran, if it succeeds in acquiring a nuclear weapons capability, "will simply take control" of maritime energy resources – something that would be potentially catastrophic for Qatar's economic security.[138]

A parallel irritant over the past quarter century has been the Qatari government's hosting of U.S. forces at the al-Udeid air base as part of its evolving relationship with Washington. This arrangement has progressively

---

135 See, for instance, Maziar Motamedi, "Iran, Qatar sign major agreements on Raisi's Doha trip," *Al-Jazeera*, February 23, 2022, https://www.aljazeera.com/news/2022/2/23/irans-president-raisi-says-14-agreements-signed-in-qatar.

136 "Iran to 'pursue rights' over disputed gas field: State media," *Al-Jazeera*, July 30, 2023, https://www.aljazeera.com/news/2023/7/30/iran-to-pursue-rights-over-disputed-gas-field-state-media.

137 Author's interviews, Doha, Qatar, May 2024.

138 Ibid.

drawn Qatar into the increasingly overt conflict between Iran and American ally Israel. For instance, al-Udeid served as a hub for the successful Western response to the large-scale salvo of drones, ballistic and cruise missiles fired by Iran at Israel in April 2024. In turn, Iranian officials have become increasingly pointed in their threats toward the country. Thus, in December of 2024, an influential Iranian diplomat, Mohammad Marandi, warned publicly that Qatar's role as a military partner of the United States will make it a target of Iranian retaliation in the event of a strike on the Islamic Republic's nuclear facilities.[139] (Notably, this did not happen when, in the summer of 2025, the United States joined in Israel's military offensive against Iran's nuclear program.)

Exploiting Afghanistan

Ties between Iran and neighboring Afghanistan have existed for millennia, with the country controlled in whole or in part by many of the Persian empires of antiquity. These include the Achaemenids, who expanded control over the territory following their ascent in 550 BC,[140] and subsequently the Sasanians, who ruled over most of it from 270 AD onward.[141] When the Safavids thereafter assumed power in 1502, they moved quickly to exert control over the entirety of Afghan territory, and wrest control of key parts of it from competing conquerors (like the Khanate of Bukhara). As a result of this extensive historic interplay, Afghanistan is portrayed in classical Iranian literature as an integral part of Persian culture and identity.

In the modern era, the two countries maintained largely pacific relations until the rise of sectarian tensions in the 1970s. In 1921, they even inked a treaty of friendship – one that was subsequently reinforced in 1935, during the reign of Zahir Shah in Kabul and Reza Shah Pahlavi in Tehran. Relations remained more or less stable until 1979, when Khomeini's Islamic

---

139 "Prominent Iranian figure threatens to destroy Qatar," *Iran International*, December 13, 2024, https://www.iranintl.com/en/202412143379.

140 "Map: The Achaemenid Empire, c. 500 BCE," *World History Encyclopedia*, n.d., https://www.worldhistory.org/uploads/images/16107.png?v=1711511463-1706686944.

141 Simon Netchev, "Map of the Sassanid Empire c. 620 CE, *World History Encyclopedia*, January 10, 2023, https://www.worldhistory.org/image/16853/the-sassanid-empire-c-620-ce/.

Revolution swept over Iran and, shortly thereafter, the Soviet Union carried out an invasion of Afghanistan to depose the country's president, Hafizullah Amin, installing a puppet government in his stead.

The new Shi'a clerical regime in Iran viewed Sunni-majority Afghanistan with suspicion, all the more so because the outbreak of the Afghan *jihad* against the Soviets that year transformed the country into an epicenter of Sunni Islamism. However, during the 1980s, Iran was preoccupied by its own protracted conflict against Iraq. And, following the Soviet ouster in 1989, Afghanistan descended into years-long civil war – culminating in the rise to power of the Taliban in 1996. The Taliban's anti-Iranian sectarian worldview dramatically worsened relations between the two countries, leading Iran to support the opposition Northern Alliance in the 1990s. While that backing proved unsuccessful, the Taliban's removal as a result of America's post-September 11th "War on Terror" created a strategic opening for Tehran, as did the weakness of the U.S.-backed Afghan government that was established in the years that followed.

The Iranian regime exploited Kabul's limited capabilities and credibility to position itself as a key power broker in Afghanistan's west. It did so by insinuating itself into local politics, as well as by operating asymmetrically throughout the country via sympathetic politicians and proxies.[142] This erosion of Afghanistan's sovereignty was facilitated by the 900-kilometer border between the two countries, which provided the Islamic Republic with a broad front from which to influence the internal affairs of its eastern neighbor, especially among the 10-15 percent of the Afghan population that is Shi'a.[143]

Those frictions persist. While their shared territorial border is relatively well demarcated and stable, the two countries have long had competing claims over shared water resources, specifically the Helmand River. These disputes, which date back more than 150 years, have resulted in sporadic

---

142   Scott Worden, "Iran and Afghanistan's Long, Complicated History," United States Institute of Peace, June 14, 2018, https://www.usip.org/publications/2018/06/iran-and-afghanistans-long-complicated-history.

143   See, for instance, Farzin Nadimi, "Iran Sets Its Eyes on Afghanistan," Washington Institute *PolicyWatch* 3513, July 19, 2021, https://www.washingtoninstitute.org/policy-analysis/iran-sets-its-eyes-afghanistan.

tensions and even outbreaks of violence – the latest of them as recently as 2023, when clashes between the two sides left one Taliban soldier and two Iranian military personnel dead.[144] Subsequent deconfliction talks appear to have reached a settlement over the waterway, at least for now.[145]

Yet Tehran continues to harbor designs over Afghanistan's larger strategic direction. Those designs have intensified since the return to power of the Taliban in the wake of the Biden administration's 2021 withdrawal from the country. To that end, Hassan Kazemi Qomi, Iran's special envoy to Afghanistan, in an attempt to woo Kabul's returned Islamists, publicly made the case in February of 2024 that Afghanistan represented part of the Iranian regime's "Axis of Resistance" against the West.[146]

Azerbaijan: A People Divided

Prior to the 1800s, the territory of what is today Azerbaijan was an integral component of successive Persian empires, and its major urban centers important outposts of imperial control. In the 19th century, however, the Qajar dynasty faced a challenge to its control over the area from an expanding Russian empire. The ensuing Russo-Persian Wars (1804-1813 and 1826-1828) resulted in two treaties – the 1813 Treaty of Gulistan and the 1828 Treaty of Turkmenchai – that ceded parts of the North Caucasus to Moscow. This effectively bifurcated the ethnic Azeri population, leading to a point of friction that persists to this day.

Thereafter, Azerbaijan was controlled first by the Russian empire and then, after the 1917 Bolshevik Revolution, by the Soviet Union. Notably, during the course of World War II, Soviet troops occupied northern Iran for several years, before being beaten back by Iranian and Allied forces, contributing to the fissure between the two constituent parts of Azerbai-

---

144 Holly Dagres, "Iran and Afghanistan are feuding over the Helmand River. The water wars have no end in sight," Atlantic Council *IranSource*, July 7, 2023, https://www.atlanticcouncil.org/blogs/iransource/iran-afghanistan-taliban-water-helmand/.

145 "Iran Claims Oral Agreement Reached With Taliban On Water Dispute," *Iran International*, November 11, 2023, https://www.iranintl.com/en/202311115804.

146 "Iran's Envoy To Kabul Sees Afghanistan As Part Of Tehran's 'Axis Of Resistance,'" *Radio Free Europe/Radio Liberty*, February 7, 2024, https://www.rferl.org/a/iran-aghanistan-envoy-qomi-axix-resistance-israel-gaza/32809698.html.

jan.[147] With the dissolution of the USSR in 1991, Azerbaijan declared its independence and plotted an independent foreign policy course – one that has put it increasingly at odds with Tehran in the years since.

Ethnic and sectarian tensions between the two countries have persisted. Estimates of the true size of Iran's Azeri population differ considerably. Conservative tallies put the figure at around 16 percent of the total Iranian population (or 14.8 million of Iran's 92.5 million people) – that is, more than the entire 10.3 million person population of the Republic of Azerbaijan.[148] Others, however, put it at far higher: perhaps as much as 25-30 million souls, or between 27 percent and 32 percent of Iran's total population.[149] All this has made influence over Azerbaijan a cardinal priority for the Islamic Republic and led the Iranian regime to interfere repeatedly in the internal affairs of its northern neighbor.[150]

Geopolitically, Azerbaijan's growing proximity to the United States, as well as to the State of Israel, in recent years has put it at fundamental odds with Iran. These tensions have been exacerbated by growing speculation about Azerbaijan's prospective entry into the "Abraham Accords" and growing signs of warming ties between the two countries, which have intensified tensions between Azerbaijan and its southern neighbor and increased the risk of conflict between the two countries.

These divisions have led Iran to seek to erode Azerbaijan's sovereignty and regional status, both directly (through domestic interference) and indirectly, by backing Baku's regional rival, Armenia, in the longstanding conflict between the two countries over the enclave of Nagorno-Karabagh. In turn, Azerbaijan's successes in the 2020 war over the territory have allowed Baku to consolidate control there, impacting Iran's trade links to Armenia and sparking fresh border tensions between Iran and its northern

---

147   See, among other sources, Gary R. Hess, "The Iranian Crisis of 1945-46 and the Cold War," *Political Science Quarterly* 89, no. 1 (March 1974), 117-146.

148   See, for instance, "Azeris in Iran," Minority Rights Group, December 2017, https://minorityrights.org/communities/azeris-2/.

149   Ariel Kogan, "Tehran's 'new old fear': Southern Azerbaijan wants independence," *i24 News*, March 2, 2023, https://www.i24news.tv/en/news/middle-east/iran-eastern-states/1677754384-iran-s-new-old-fear-southern-azerbaijan-wants-independence.

150   For a more detailed examination of these activities, see Ilan Berman, *Tehran Rising: Iran's Challenge to the United States* (Lanham, MD: Rowman & Littlefield, 2005), 94-96.

neighbor.[151] While this has not yet led to conflict between Baku and Tehran, the potential for hostilities remains. This is particularly so given Tehran's unease regarding Azerbaijan's pro-Western political tilt. It is also due to the fact that, in the words of regional officials, Iran's clerical regime views the modern-day independence of Azerbaijan as something akin to an "accident of history."[152]

Navigating a New Era of Weakness

Iran's regional ambitions, as well as its strategic position, have experienced dramatic shifts in the past two years.

On October 7, 2023, its main Palestinian proxy, Hamas, carried out an unprecedented campaign of terror against civilian communities in southern Israel. The group's large-scale incursion into the country resulted in the largest slaughter of Jews since the Holocaust and precipitated a new phase of the Israeli-Palestinian confrontation.

There is still an ongoing debate over the extent of the role played by Iran in masterminding the massacre. It is clear, however, that in a very real sense the Islamic Republic served as its enabler. "Iran has funded, armed, trained, and provided intelligence to Hamas for decades," Matthew Levitt of the Washington Institute has explained. "Iran's terrorist training programs, and its consistent effort to arm Hamas over the years, are the reason Hamas has been able to carry out attacks targeting Israel including the October 7 massacre."[153]

What is unquestionable is that the terror campaign perpetrated by Hamas was broadly consonant with Iranian strategic interests. The events of that day, at least temporarily, dented the image of Israel as an unassailable, formidable strategic power – something policymakers in Jerusalem had

151   See, for instance, Anna Borshchevskaya and Andrew Tabler, "Iran's Tensions with Azerbaijan Point to Broader Shifts in the South Caucasus," Washington Institute *PolicyWatch* no. 3726, March 31, 2023, https://www.washingtoninstitute.org/policy-analysis/irans-tensions-azerbaijan-point-broader-shifts-south-caucasus.
152   Author's interview, Tel Aviv, Israel, May 2025.
153   Matthew Levitt, "The Hamas-Iran Relationship," *Jerusalem Strategic Tribune*, November 2023, https://jstribune.com/levitt-the-hamas-iran-relationship/.

worked diligently to establish for decades. Thereafter, the military offensive launched by Israel in the Gaza Strip helped isolate Jerusalem on the world stage, short-circuit Israel's normalization efforts with the countries of the "Abraham Accords," and inject new friction into the "special relationship" between Israel and the United States.[154]

Beginning in September 2024, however, the strategic balance began to shift decisively against the Islamic Republic. Israel's decision to open a "northern front" against Hezbollah in southern Lebanon yielded rapid, dramatic results. These included the killing or crippling of thousands of the group's mid-level military commanders, as well as the death of its leader, Hassan Nasrallah. It also entailed the elimination of an estimated 80 percent of the group's extensive arsenal of short- and medium-range rockets, which over the previous decade had been used by Iran (via the group) to establish a "balance of terror" with the Jewish state and foreclose the possibility of resolute Israeli military action against its nuclear program. Simultaneously, Israel's late-October 2024 reprisal attack against Iran (a response to Iranian ballistic missile strikes earlier that month) had a devastating effect, eliminating the Iranian regime's air defense capabilities and demonstrating Jerusalem's capacity to extensively target the Islamic Republic. These developments have, in the words of one seasoned observer, demonstrated to the world that "the Ayatollah has no clothes."[155]

Iran has lost ground on another front as well. The December 2024 ouster of Syrian dictator Bashar al-Assad at the hands of Sunni opposition forces represented a grievous strategic blow to Tehran – one that has impacted Iran's imperial ambitions in a material way, interrupting the so-called "land bridge" that the regime had for years used to ferry weapons and war material from its territory to assorted proxies in Syria and Lebanon.

All this has collectively brought the Iranian regime to its weakest point in decades. As a result, the Islamic Republic is now shifting its strategy, and attempting to advance its objectives, and its imperialism, by other means.

---

154   Ilan Berman, "Israel's New War Is Part Of Iran's Strategic Plan." *The National Interest*, October 20, 2023, https://nationalinterest.org/blog/buzz/israels-new-war-part-irans-strategic-plan-206993.

155   Interview with Rich Goldberg, *Call Me Back podcast*, October 29, 2024, https://podcasts.apple.com/us/podcast/the-ayatollah-has-no-clothes-with-rich-goldberg/id1539292794?i=1000674810980.

In a December 2024 article in *Foreign Affairs*, Iranian Vice President for Strategic Affairs Mohammad Javad Zarif laid out a political vision for regional cooperation, the eviction of external powers (like the United States), and the destruction of the State of Israel. At the heart of Zarif's proposal is the idea of a "new regional arrangement that reduces the Persian Gulf's reliance on external powers and encourages stakeholders to address conflicts through dispute resolution mechanisms."[156] Embedded in this idea is the understanding that the Iranian regime would dominate any such construct – in effect establishing the *Pax Irannica* that Tehran has long sought to establish in the region.

---

156   Mohammad Javad Zarif, "How Iran Sees the Path to Peace," *Foreign Affairs*, December 2, 2024, https://www.foreignaffairs.com/iran/how-iran-sees-path-peace.

The Fellow Travelers: North Korea and Venezuela

In their current attempts to remake the world order, Beijing, Moscow and Tehran are not alone. Today's new imperialists can rely on the practical assistance and political support of a pair of ideological fellow travelers. These actors – the brutal Kim dynasty of North Korea and the radical leftist regime that runs Venezuela – have gravitated to the shared mission now being pursued by all three nations: to refashion the global rules of the road to their benefit, and to the great detriment of the West.

Each has done so in its own ways, ranging from military support to strategic assistance. These interactions are extensive, and a comprehensive treatment remains well beyond the scope of this work. However, the abbreviated histories below highlight how these actors have become enablers for the parallel imperial quests of Xi's China, Putin's Russia and Khamenei's Iran. In turn, their partnerships with Beijing, Moscow and Tehran have helped fuel their own ambitions, with potentially dire consequences for their respective regions in the years ahead.

North Korea

In today's wired, interconnected world, the Democratic People's Republic of Korea (DPRK) represents an anachronism. An insular one-party state ruled by a hereditary dynasty and intentionally cut off from modernity, North

Korea is a "black box" of sorts for intelligence analysis that has frustrated informed policymaking in the West for decades.

The modern-day DPRK emerged out of the post-World War II division of the Korean Peninsula following Japanese colonial rule. With the retraction of Japanese power, the Soviet Union orchestrated the installation of former guerrilla Kim Il Sung as the country's leader – setting it on a course of protracted familial rule. The subsequent establishment, in 1948, of the DPRK saw Kim installed as Premier. Shortly thereafter, the ideology of *Juche* – centering on self-reliance, fealty to the state, and the centrality of the national leader – was enshrined as its guiding ethos.

From its start, however, North Korea has been a revisionist state, undergirded by a maximalist, expansionist vision that posits itself as the natural inheritor of the Korean peninsula. As the scholar Daniel Pinkston has explained, "In the official conception of the state, the territory of the DPRK includes the whole Korean peninsula and its surrounding islands, and the DPRK represents the interests of all the Korean people." [157] This, in turn, has meant that officials in Pyongyang see the neighboring Republic of Korea (ROK) as an illegitimate entity – a view that has helped animate the DPRK's decades-long efforts to subvert South Korean sovereignty.

Over the decades, the Kim family – Kim Il Sung (1948-1994), his son Kim Jong-il (1994-2011), and current "dear leader" Kim Jong Un (2011 to present) – has sought to ensure the survival of its "pure" socialist regime in various ways. At home, this has meant isolating itself from the world. What limited literature there exists on the absurdist, warped nature of the "Hermit Kingdom" details a regime that has intentionally cut itself off from international progress, where the ruling party wields unchecked state power, where surveillance is pervasive, and where the consequences of political and social non-conformity range from torture to mass imprisonment to disappearance and collective punishment.[158]

Over the past seven decades, these deformities have made North Korea

---

157   Daniel Pinkston, "The Asymmetric Strategies of the DPRK," in Ilan Berman, ed., *The Logic of Irregular War: Asymmetric Warfare and America's Adversaries* (Lanham, MD: Rowman & Littlefield, 2017), 90.

158   See, for instance, Barbara Demick, *Nothing to Envy: Ordinary Lives in North Korea* (New York: Random House, 2010).

a source of considerable international concern and opprobrium.[159] Yet the DPRK is not simply a menace to its own captive population. It has also become a truly global threat, in large part because of its parallel partnerships with the PRC, Russia and the Islamic Republic of Iran.

Pyongyang and the PRC

Sino-Korean relations date back to antiquity, owing to the geographical proximity of the Middle Kingdom and the Chosun peninsula. Trade and migration from China helped shape early Korean political and technological development, while the influence of successive Chinese dynasties imported Confucian thought, Chinese writing and administrative organization to the assorted Korean kingdoms. Over the centuries, this long-term interaction transformed Korea into a diplomatic tributary and cultural outpost.

The twin founding of the People's Republic of China and Democratic People's Republic of Korea led to a temporary communist alliance. Beijing intervened in support of the North during the ensuing Korean war, providing Pyongyang with economic and military assistance against U.S.-led forces. At that time, China saw Korea as the vanguard against Western capitalist encroachment, as well as an important security buffer.[160] Thereafter, during the decades of the Cold War, contacts and overall Chinese support continued, notwithstanding the entrenchment of *Juche* ideology, with its prioritization of self-reliance.

The trend has remained unchanged in the post-Cold War era, despite the emergence of issues, like North Korea's nuclear program, on which Pyongyang and Beijing have differed. And with the rise to power of Xi Jinping in 2013, the two countries have launched a new era of enhanced contacts.

Contemporary Sino-Korean ties can be categorized in a number of

---

159   See, for instance, U.S. Department of State, Bureau of Democracy, Human Rights, and Labor, *2023 Country Reports on Human Rights Practices*, April 2024, https://www.state.gov/reports/2023-country-reports-on-human-rights-practices/.

160   Amy Hawkins and Helen Davidson, "North Korea's involvement in Ukraine draws China into a delicate balancing act," *The Guardian*, November 6, 2024, https://www.theguardian.com/world/2024/nov/06/north-korea-troops-russia-ukraine-war-china-relationship.

ways. Economically, China is the DPRK's predominant trading partner, representing the overwhelming majority (some 98%) of its official trade.[161] China has also facilitated the North Korean regime's access to global markets, in spite of the extensive international sanctions levied against Pyongyang, through measures like the employment of North Korean laborers and assorted schemes for sanctions evasion.[162]

Politically, the two sides continue to generally coordinate on international affairs. The year 2024, which marked 75 years of collaboration, was officially dubbed the "Year of Sino-North Korea Friendship" and punctuated by diplomatic exchanges of letters and joint commitments to cooperation. Nevertheless, tensions are now evident in the relationship. Pyongyang's growing proximity to Russia – and its active support of the Russian government's war on Ukraine –has injected some tension into its bilateral relationship with Beijing.

This, scholars note, is logical. "Since its founding, North Korea has typically been close to either the Soviet Union (and now Russia) or China — not both," Choong-Koo Lee of the Korean Institute for Defense Analyses has explained.[163] Now that North Korea's policy "pendulum" has swung in favor of closer ties with the Kremlin, the vibrancy of its partnership with the PRC has naturally suffered. Nevertheless, bilateral ties have not suffered meaningfully as a result.

The Pyongyang-Moscow Connection

Today, the DPRK's assistance to Russia's war of aggression against Ukraine has become a major focus of international attention. Since mid-2024, the regime of Kim Jong-un in Pyongyang has become a major participant in the

---

161 Jihoon Lee, "North Korea's economy surged in 2023 after years of contraction, South estimates," Reuters, July 25, 2024, https://www.reuters.com/markets/asia/north-koreas-economy-surged-2023-after-years-contraction-south-estimates-2024-07-26/.

162 Edward Howell, "North Korea and Russia's dangerous partnership: The China factor," Chatham House research paper, December 4, 2024, https://www.chathamhouse.org/2024/12/north-korea-and-russias-dangerous-partnership/china-factor.

163 Choong-Koo Lee, "China's Ties with North Korea are in a Ditch, and Therein Lies Opportunity," War on the Rocks, February 19, 2025, https://warontherocks.com/2025/02/chinas-ties-with-north-korea-are-in-a-ditch-and-therin-lies-opportunity/.

conflict through its provision of battlefield weaponry, ranging from artillery shells to ballistic missiles.[164] It has also sent an estimated 14,000 soldiers to date to help Russia reinforce its front lines, as well as to turn back Ukrainian incursions into Russian territory.[165] In this way, North Korea has helped to alleviate the chronic manpower shortages that have bedeviled Russia's war effort.[166]

In exchange for this support, North Korea has been rewarded handsomely. According to intelligence assessments, the Kremlin has likely helped the DPRK to develop a new air-to-air missile,[167] aided the construction of the country's fleet of next generation drones,[168] and assisted the creation of the country's newest warship.[169] The two sides have also signed a treaty on "comprehensive strategic partnership," which codifies bilateral coordination in the event one party is threatened, as well as prompt military assistance to support the other in the face of external threats.[170]

In truth, however, the contemporary Russian-North Korean relationship is far more extensive and longer-lasting than simply the current round of wartime cooperation. The dissolution of the USSR led to a significant deterioration in ties between Moscow and Pyongyang, including the abrogation, in 1991, of the 1961 Treaty of Friendship, Cooperation and Mutual Assistance between the DPRK and the USSR by then-Russian President Boris Yeltsin.[171] In its place, Moscow expanded its outreach to Seoul and sought to forge economic and political ties to South Korea. But the estrangement proved merely temporary. Beginning in the early 2000s,

---

164 Catherine Kim, "The North Korea-Russia alliance gets tighter," *Politico*, May 22, 2025, https://www.politico.com/newsletters/politico-nightly/2025/05/22/the-north-korea-russia-alliance-gets-tighter-00366472.

165 Joel Guinto and Jean Mackenzie, "N Korea confirms it sent troops to fight for Russia in Ukraine war," *BBC*, April 27, 2025, https://www.bbc.com/news/articles/ckg25wxvpy2o; Harvey, "North Korea has sent 3,000 more soldiers to bolster Russia's war on Ukraine, South Korea says."

166 See, for instance, Pavel Luzin, "Russia's year of truth: the soldier shortage," Center for European Policy Analysis, January 22, 2025, https://cepa.org/article/russias-year-of-truth-1-the-soldier-shortage/.

167 Kim, "The North Korea-Russia alliance gets tighter."

168 Ibid.

169 Tom Porter, "North Korea's new warship may have been aided by Russian tech, and it's a worrying development," *Business Insider*, April 29, 2025, https://www.businessinsider.com/north-korea-new-warship-choe-hyon-aided-russia-tech-concern-2025-4.

170 See, for instance, Tessa Wong, "Putin and Kim pledge mutual help against 'aggression,'" *BBC*, June 19, 2024, https://www.bbc.com/news/articles/ceddqkqzd5wo.

171 Gilbert Rozman, *The Strategic Triangle: China, the United States, and the Future of East Asian Security* (M.E. Sharpe, 2007).

Russia – now under the leadership of Vladimir Putin – sought to reengage with the DPRK. This included growing Russian support for North Korea in multilateral venues (including the so-called "Six Party Talks" over North Korea's nuclear program).[172]

Economically, meanwhile, Russia steadily emerged as a major lifeline for the Kim regime. In 2012, Russia forgave an estimated 90% of the DPRK's Soviet-era debt, totaling approximately $11 billion.[173] Russia also emerged as a significant destination for North Korean labor, with workers from the DPRK traveling to the Russian Far East to seek employment in sectors such as construction and energy. The revenues thereby generated have served as a "windfall" for the Kim regime, helping it to weather the economic downturn of recent years.[174] Russia's government, for its part, has been happy to flout UN Security Council sanctions, issued in 2020, which have sought to bar member states from hosting North Korean workers.[175] (This cooperation, moreover, appears to be expanding; amid the ongoing Ukraine war, the number of laborers being sent by North Korea has surged – suggesting that the DPRK's assistance to the Kremlin in its attempts to conquer Kyiv includes a financial reward for Pyongyang.[176])

Ties between Russia and the DPRK, in other words are strong – and getting stronger in spite of international pressure on both. Or perhaps precisely because of it.

---

172 Michael J. Mazarr, *North Korea and the Bomb: A Case Study in Nonproliferation* (St. Martin's Press, 1997).

173 Maya Dyakina and Lidia Kelly, "Russia writes off 90 percent of North Korea's debt," Reuters, September 18, 2012, https://www.reuters.com/article/us-korea-north-debt/russia-writes-off-90-percent-of-north-koreas-debt-idUSBRE88H0NH20120918/.

174 Isabelle Khurshudyan and Min Joo Kim, "For North Korean workers, Russia's Far East remains a windfall for them and for Kim's regime," *Washington Post*, July 18, 2021, https://koreajoongangdaily.joins.com/news/2025-02-05/national/northKorea/North-Koreans-entering-Russia-surge-to-13000-suggests-labor-deal-amid-Ukraine-war-/2235761.

175 Ibid.

176 Seo Ji-eun, "North Koreans entering Russia surge to 13,000, suggests labor deal amid Ukraine war," *Korea JoonAng Daily*, February 5, 2025, https://koreajoongangdaily.joins.com/news/2025-02-05/national/northKorea/North-Koreans-entering-Russia-surge-to-13000-suggests-labor-deal-amid-Ukraine-war-/2235761.

North Korea and Iran: Birds of a Feather

The strategic partnership between North Korea and Iran is a comparatively recent phenomenon, in historical terms. To be sure, imperial Iran and the Korean peninsula had indirect links in antiquity via the vaunted Silk Road, which created a degree of commerce between the two.[177] But it wasn't until 1979 and the Islamic Revolution that North Korea's Stalinist regime forged an alliance with the country's new clerical order. At that time, Iran – now isolated from its traditional partner, the United States – sought new suppliers for its military aims. Together with the Soviet Union and Communist China, the DPRK emerged as a major source of arms for the fledgling Islamic Republic. That dependence deepened in the years that followed, as Iran became embroiled in a costly eight-year conflict with neighboring Iraq.[178] The Kim regime gradually took on the role of a major military supplier for that campaign, providing Iran with a wide array of weapons, including missiles.[179]

Those early contacts were underpinned by an ideological meeting of the minds. For all the differences in their respective ideologies, both nations saw themselves as revolutionary, revisionist states. They also shared an antipathy to what they viewed as Western imperialism, laying the groundwork for what would develop into a thriving strategic partnership.[180]

This synergy took the form, most conspicuously, of cooperation on ballistic missiles. Beginning in the 1990s, the DPRK became instrumental to the development of Iran's now-formidable arsenal of medium-range missiles. This has included joint testing and development, as well as the reverse-engineering of North Korea's *No Dong* into the mainstay of Iran's contemporary ballistic missile arsenal, the *Shahab 3*.[181] North Korea is also

---

177   See, for instance, UNESCO, "Did you know?: Gyeongju and the Silk Roads," n.d., https://en.unesco. org/silkroad/content/did-you-know-gyeongju-and-silk-roads.

178   Christina Y. Lin, "China, Iran, and North Korea: A Triangular Strategic Alliance," *Middle East Review of International Affairs*, March 2010, https://www.scribd.com/document/51876158/ China-Iran-Alliance.

179   Ibid.

180   See generally Bruce Bechtol, *Defiant Failed State: The North Korean Threat to International Security* (Washington, DC: Potomac Books, 2010).

181   See, for instance, Michael Elleman, "North Korea-Iran Missile Cooperation," *38 North*, September 22, 2016, https://www.38north.org/2016/09/melleman092216/.

known to have helped Iran in the development of intercontinental-range ballistic missiles,[182] thereby becoming a key contributor to the missile threat that the Islamic Republic poses to the West.

But the interaction between the two countries extends further still. Both are known to have benefited from the transfer of nuclear know-how by Pakistan's notorious AQ Khan,[183] and circumstantial evidence points to significant – albeit clandestine – contacts relating to their respective atomic programs.[184] North Korea has also played a material role in helping the Islamic Republic skirt sanctions imposed by the United States and the international community. Due to its international isolation, the DPRK has come to depend heavily on illicit financial networks and covert trade in order to remain (mostly) solvent. Predictably, this gray- and black-market activity has been harnessed by the Iranian regime to dilute the effectiveness of the international sanctions that have been levied on it over the past quarter-century for its nuclear work and support for international terrorism. Through a range of methods – from money laundering to the clandestine transfer of oil and other goods – North Korea has become an indispensable partner for the Islamic Republic.[185]

Pyongyang has also become enmeshed in Iran's network of radical proxies. A significant number of Hezbollah operatives are said to have received training in the DPRK in years past, and the North Korean regime allegedly helped the Lebanese Shi'a militia construct a network of tunnels by which to penetrate into Israel and clandestinely move men and material in southern Lebanon.[186] The Kim regime has also maintained a long-standing relationship with the Palestinian Hamas movement, one which has included

182   Bill Gertz, "Iran, North Korea Secretly Developing New Long Range Rocket Booster for ICBMs," *Washington Free Beacon*, November 26, 2013, https://freebeacon.com/national-security/iran-north-korea-secretly-developing-new-long-range-rocket-booster-for-icbms/.

183   See generally William Langewiesche, *The Atomic Bazaar: Dispatches from the Underground World of Nuclear Trafficking* (New York: Farrar, Straus and Giroux, 2008).

184   See, for instance, "Source: Hundreds of NK Nuclear and Missile Experts Working in Iran," *Korea Times*, November 13, 2011, https://www.koreatimes.co.kr/southkorea/20111113/source-hundreds-of-nk-nuclear-and-missile-experts-working-in-iran.

185   United Against Nuclear Iran, "Iran & North Korea: Proliferation Partners," June 2024, https://www.unitedagainstnucleariran.com/north-korea-iran.

186   Samuel Ramani, "North Korea's Covert Alliance With Iran Aligned Militias in the Middle East," *38 North*, October 23, 2023, https://www.38north.org/2023/10/north-koreas-covert-alliance-with-iran-aligned-militias-in-the-middle-east/

"weapons transfers, financial assistance, and training" – as well as help in the creation of the "Gaza Metro," the elaborate web of tunnels and passageways underneath the Gaza Strip that has become central to the group's resilience since October 7, 2023.[187] North Korea has also had substantial contacts with Yemen's Houthi rebels, most conspicuously by facilitating missile transfers to the Iranian proxy group.[188]

In these ways, Pyongyang has helped to bolster Iran's great power ambitions, and to expand the threat that both the Iranian regime and its vast network of radical proxies pose to the Middle East, and beyond.

Persistent Dreams of Reunification

Notably, North Korea's assistance to Russia, China and Iran has whetted the DPRK's own imperial appetite. Ever since the 1953 armistice that ended the active phase of the Korean civil war, Pyongyang has looked for ways to conquer South Korea. Historian and Korea watcher Daniel Pinkston has made the case that this yearning is rooted in North Korean strategic culture, as well as representing a manifestation of the ideology of the Kim dynasty, which sees itself as the natural inheritor of the Korean Peninsula as a whole.[189]

Indeed, as long ago as 1973, then-North Korean Leader Kim Il Sung was already promoting his "Three principles of national unification," which envisioned the peaceful reunification of the Peninsula under Pyongyang's control.[190] Subsequently, in 1993, Kim expanded his views into a "ten point programme" designed to promote the "great unity" of the Koreas.[191] Upon

---

187 Ellen Kim and Salamata Bah, "The DPRK-Hamas Relationship," Center for Strategic and International Studies, March 27, 2024, https://www.csis.org/analysis/dprk-hamas-relationship.

188 See, for instance, Ramani, "North Korea's Covert Alliance With Iran Aligned Militias in the Middle East."

189 Daniel Pinkston, "The Asymmetric Strategies of the DPRK," in Ilan Berman, ed., *The Logic of Irregular War: Asymmetric Warfare and America's Adversaries* (Lanham, MD: Rowman & Littlefield, 2017), 90.

190 Kim Il Sung, "On The Three Principles of National Unification," May 3 and November 3, 1972, https://kkfonline.com/wp-content/uploads/2020/04/On-The-Three-Principles-Of-National-Reunification.pdf.

191 Kim Il Sung, "Ten-Point Programme of the Great Unity of the Whole Nation for the Reunification of the Country," April 6, 1993, https://nautilus.org/publications/books/dprkbb/aboutdprk/dprk-briefing-book-dprk-history/ten-point-programme-of-the-great-unity-of-the-whole-nation-for-the-reunification-of-the-country/.

the elder Kim's death in 1994, the mission of reunification was taken up by his son and successor, Kim Jong-il. And when, upon his subsequent death, his son Kim Jong Un assumed power, he made it a priority as well. In his first public address as North Korea's ruler in April 2012, Kim Jong Un extolled the "historic cause of the fatherland's reunification."[192]

Over time, however, this objective has shifted. As its strategic capabilities have strengthened, thanks to its partnership with the regimes in Beijing, Moscow and Tehran, North Korea's rhetoric has hardened. In early 2024, Kim called publicly for the revision of the country's constitution to designate the South as his country's "primary foe" and "principal enemy." He also suggested that the constitutional amendments include plans for "occupying, subjugating and reclaiming" South Korea in the event of a future war between the two sides.[193] This rhetorical shift suggests a strategic reorientation in Pyongyang underpinned by the belief that reunification cannot be accomplished absent force of arms. Meanwhile, the DPRK's own expanded capabilities —courtesy of its partnership with China, Russia and Iran of recent years – make it more capable than ever of attaining such an outcome.

Venezuela

Like North Korea under the Kim regime, present-day Venezuela ranks as a fundamentally revisionist state. Over the past half-century, the South American nation has transitioned from relative stability to radical socialism as the political power-sharing arrangements enshrined in the 1958 Puntofijo Pact gave way to Hugo Chavez's strongman politics in the late 1990s. Indeed, the May 1998 election of Chavez, a former military officer and failed coup plotter, to the Venezuelan presidency marked a radical refashioning of the state. Venezuela's new president presided over a new constitution, passed the following year, which enshrined a vision of Bolivarian Revolution based

---

192   "Kim Jong-un's first public speech," *North Korean Economy Watch*, April 15, 2012, https://www.nkeconwatch.com/2012/04/15/kim-jong-uns-first-public-speech/.

193   "North Korea Ends Policy of Reunification with South Korea," *Voice of America*, January 16, 2024, https://www.voanews.com/a/north-korea-ends-policy-of-reunification-with-south-korea/7441790.html.

on the tenets of Simon Bolivar, the 19th century Venezuelan-born political leader who advocated for a continent free of imperial control. It also dramatically expanded the powers of the presidency, providing Chavez with the freedom to pursue his national and foreign policy priorities.

This embrace of leftist ideology made Venezuela a natural ally of forces seeking to subvert the Western-led order.[194] First under Chavez, who ruled until his death from cancer in March 2013, and subsequently under that of his hand-picked successor Nicolas Maduro, Caracas has drifted into alignment with the burgeoning anti-Western alliance being erected by China, Russia and Iran, even as its domestic situation has deteriorated. In turn, collaboration with the neo-imperial regimes in Beijing, Moscow and Tehran has led the Maduro regime, despite its current political difficulties, to seek to expand its own reach and power in the Americas.

A Thriving Sino-Venezuelan Alignment

Ties between Venezuela and China have existed for half-a-century. The two formally established diplomatic relations in June of 1974, after the government of then-Venezuelan president Carlos Perez made the decision to sever its ties to Taiwan. That shift was precipitated by Venezuela's efforts, under Perez, to position itself as a leader of the non-aligned movement, as well as growing recognition in Caracas of the economic opportunities that could be had by embracing the much larger PRC.[195] The move paved the way for the development of what is today an extensive – and ongoing – collaboration that stretches across multiple domains.

Economically, energy-rich Venezuela has now been a key supplier of crude to China for some three decades, beginning in the 1990s when growing demand for oil caused the PRC to look farther and farther afield to fuel its economic growth.[196] The advent of the Chavez regime in 1998,

---

194　See generally Jon B. Purdue, *The War of all the People: The Nexus of Latin American Radicalism and Middle Eastern Terrorism* (Washington, DC: Potomac Books, 2012).

195　Richard Gott, *Hugo Chávez and the Bolivarian Revolution* (New York: Verso, 2005)

196　Andrew Hayley, "China's oil trade and investment in Venezuela," Reuters, September 12, 2023, https://www.reuters.com/business/energy/chinas-oil-trade-investment-venezuela-2023-09-12/.

however, provided an ideological underpinning for this interaction – one that has allowed it to thrive in the years since, in spite of Western sanctions. Since 2007, China has provided the country with more than $50 billion in loans, allowing Chavez (and subsequently Maduro) to mitigate, at least somewhat, Venezuela's protracted trajectory of decline. The PRC now ranks as Venezuela's largest creditor, and its investments – mostly in the form of loan-for-oil deals that have seen Chinese banks bankroll the development of Venezuelan oil assets – have played an indispensable role in propping up the country's regime.

Politically, too, ties between the two countries have proven durable. Modest diplomatic contacts starting in the 1970s continued apace in subsequent years, though they were circumscribed by Venezuela's general alignment with the United States during the decades of the Cold War.[197] But the shift in political outlook that accompanied Chavez's rise to power created an expanded basis for cooperation, and ties intensified dramatically thereafter. This included multiple visits to China by Chavez, PRC backing for Venezuela in multilateral forums, and massive investment in the Latin American state by China's government.[198] In return, Venezuela has become a loyal adherent to China's official stances vis-à-vis Taiwan, Xinjiang and sovereignty in the South China Sea.

For its part, the strategic relationship between the two countries has grown steadily since the 2000s. It has evolved from largely symbolic defense ties into a partnership that encompasses arms sales, joint military training, intelligence collaboration and broader geopolitical coordination. China, for instance, has assisted the Maduro regime in strengthening its grip against internal opponents, supplying authorities with high-tech surveillance equipment to help track political dissent.[199] The two have also carried out regular

---

197 R. Evan Ellis, *China in Latin America: The Whats and Wherefores* (New York: Lynn Reiner, 2009).

198 Between 1999 and 2018, China is estimated to have invested over $6 billion in Venezuela, and proffered loans totaling some $62 billion. Transparencia Venezuela, "China-Venezuela: Financial, economic and production management," March 2025, https://transparenciave.org/wp-content/uploads/2025/03/China-Venezuela-Relations.-Financial-economic-and-production-management.-Transparencia-Venezuela-en-el-exilio.pdf.

199 Angus Berwick, "Special Report: How ZTE helps Venezuela create China-style social control," Reuters, November 14, 2018, https://www.reuters.com/article/technology/special-report-how-zte-helps-venezuela-create-china-style-social-control-idUSKCN1NJ1ZV/.

high-level military exchanges, and Venezuela is known to have hosted delegations of the People's Liberation Army. While no large-scale military maneuvers have taken place between the two to date, Beijing and Caracas continue to coordinate policy on foreign affairs, both bilaterally and via the BRICS bloc, of which both are members.

These ties are now poised to expand further still. In September of 2023, Presidents Xi Jinping and Nicolas Maduro elevated their longstanding cooperation into an "all-weather strategic partnership," [200] laying the basis for expanded interaction in a shared pursuit of a "multipolar world order" in which America's role is diminished, and that of Beijing, Caracas and their partners is expanded.

The Moscow-Caracas Connection

Like with China, Venezuela's relations with Russia blossomed with the ideological transformation ushered in by Hugo Chavez in the late 1990s. Before then, contacts were minimal during the Cold War era, and only hesitant in the immediate post-Cold War period. But the Venezuelan-Russian relationship entered a new phase once Chavez's explicitly anti-American, anti-imperialist ideology became the order of the day in Caracas.

During the Chavez era, Venezuela became Russia's largest Latin American arms client. Over the span of roughly two decades (between 2000 and 2020), Venezuela is estimated to have procured $20 billion in arms from the Kremlin. [201] The two also carried out an active schedule of joint military exercises. Despite the transition from Chavez to Maduro, the relationship has persisted; Venezuela continues to receive military support from Russia, as well as ongoing political backing for Maduro's continued rule despite widespread recognition that Maduro's most recent political victory was ille-

---

200   Ministry of Foreign Affairs of the People's Republic of China, "Xi Jinping Exchanges Congratulatory Messages with Venezuelan President Nicolás Maduro Moros on the 50th Anniversary of the Establishment of Diplomatic Relations between China and Venezuela," June 28, 2024, https://www.fmprc.gov.cn/eng/xw/zyxw/202407/t20240712_11453025.html.

201   Peter Cavanagh, "Russia became an important arms supplier for Latin America, but its sales have dropped," ARS Report, May 2020, https://www.unav.edu/web/global-affairs/detalle/-/blogs/russia-became-an-important-arms-supplier-for-latin-america-but-its-sales-have-dropped?utm_source=chatgpt.com.

gitimate. And in May of 2025, Presidents Putin and Maduro signed a 10 year comprehensive strategic cooperation accord, under which the two pledged an enduring partnership "to defy Western hegemony."[202] Under the new pact, Russia and Venezuela committed to expanding bilateral cooperation on energy, mutual efforts to decouple from the SWIFT financial banking system and reduce reliance on the U.S. dollar, and expanded military and defense cooperation.[203]

Economically, meanwhile, Russia and Venezuela have developed a multifaceted partnership – one that encompasses energy cooperation between Russia's ROSNEFT and Venezuela's state-owned PDVSA, as well as financial assistance in the form of loans and debt restructuring. Russia has also become involved in a number of Venezuelan infrastructure projects, as well as dipping its toe into mining and nuclear energy in the country.[204] This cooperation has proven essential to Maduro, who has increasingly sought alternatives to Western engagement as a result of sanctions on the part of the United States and Europe. With its recently signed strategic pact, this dimension of the Russian-Venezuelan partnership, like military coordination, is now poised to expand further.

The Ahmadinejad-Chavez Alliance... and Beyond

While Iran's interest in Latin America dates to the mid-1980s, when the fledgling Islamic Republic helped its main terror proxy, Hezbollah, ensconce itself in the "Tri-Border Region" at the nexus of Argentina, Brazil and Paraguay, Tehran's true presence in the region is of significantly more recent vintage. It is intimately tied to the rise of Hugo Chavez in Caracas in the late 1990s, and to the personal bonds subsequently established between him and Iranian President Mahmoud Ahmadinejad after the latter took office in Tehran in 2005.

---

202 "Inside Putin and Maduro's Historic Agreement to Defy Western Hegemony," *TeleSUR English*, May 13, 2025, https://www.telesurenglish.net/inside-putin-maduros-historic-agreement/.

203 Ibid.

204 See, for instance, "Russia to build nuclear power plant in Venezuela," Reuters, October 15, 2010, https://www.reuters.com/article/business/energy/russia-to-build-nuclear-power-plant-in-venezuela-idUSLDE69E22G/.

Iran's revolutionary pedigree made it a natural partner for Chavez as he sought to alter his country's political trajectory, while Venezuela's then still comparatively robust economy made it an attractive partner for an Iran battered by Western sanctions. Those practical benefits were augmented by deep ideological alignment, leading the two countries to forge an "axis of unity" built around anti-Americanism, a shared desire to dilute the effectiveness of Western sanctions, and revolutionary zeal.[205]

Thus, the Chavez regime assumed an important role in Iran's efforts to circumvent international sanctions, lending its banking sector and access to world markets to the Islamic Republic.[206] The two countries also forged a robust military partnership, establishing numerous joint defense-industrial projects on Venezuelan soil.[207] Venezuela also became a welcoming hub and source of support for Iran's Hezbollah, whose facilitators and fundraisers enjoyed freedom of movement within the "Bolivarian" state.[208] Perhaps most significantly, Iran used its relationship with Venezuela as a springboard to build ties to the region's other revolutionary states, among them Rafael Correa's Ecuador, the Bolivia of Evo Morales, and the regime of Daniel Ortega in Nicaragua.[209] These and assorted other developments led experts to warn that "Iran and Venezuela have forged an alliance that frays the American security blanket while constraining U.S. policy on an array of issues."[210]

All too often, however, the common understanding of the Iran-Venezuela alliance is that it is an anachronism – a product of the close personal ties between Ahmadinejad and Chavez. A corollary of that view holds that, since both leaders are no longer at the helm (Ahmadinejad ended his term in office in 2013, while Chavez succumbed to an aggressive cancer the same year), the alliance they forged is a thing of the past.

---

205 See generally Sean Goforth, *Axis of Unity: Venezuela, Iran & the Threat to America* (Washington, DC: Potomac Books, 2012).

206 Norman A. Bailey, "Iran's Venezuelan Gateway," American Foreign Policy Council *Iran Strategy Brief* no. 5, February 2012, https://www.afpc.org/uploads/documents/ISB5.pdf.

207 For a thorough summary of this cooperation, see Martin Rodil, "A Venezuelan Platform for Iran's Military Ambitions," in Joseph Humire and Ilan Berman, eds., *Iran's Strategic Penetration of Latin America* (Lanham, MD: Lexington Books, 2014)

208 Martin Arostengui, "U.S. Ties Caracas to Hezbollah Aid," *Washington Times*, July 7, 2008, https://www.washingtontimes.com/news/2008/jul/07/us-ties-caracas-to-hezbollah-aid/.

209 See generally Humire and Berman, eds., *Iran's Strategic Penetration of Latin America*.

210 Goforth, *Axis of Unity*, xvi.

Nothing could be further from the truth. Iran's ties to Venezuela have transcended the Ahmadinejad era, with the Islamic Republic maintaining a keen interest in Latin America as a whole – and its ties to Caracas in particular. Indeed, over the past five years, Iran has intensified its engagement with the Americas, stepping up its diplomatic, economic and strategic interaction with countries in the Western Hemisphere.[211] Venezuela, Iran's oldest and most dependable regional partner, remains the lynchpin of its regional strategy, which is focused on countering American influence, building economic partnerships, and expanding its radical ideology beyond its borders.

The Dream of Greater Venezuela

Notably, Venezuela's links to China, Russia and Iran have helped empower its own, local version of imperial revanchism. At the center of these yearnings is the Essequibo, a resource-rich region that encompasses some two-thirds of the territory of neighboring Guyana. Competing claims over the area date back to colonial times, when Venezuela (a former Spanish colony) and the British colony of Guyana each contested where their shared border should be drawn. The matter was settled via an international tribunal, which ruled in 1899 to demarcate the border along its present lines.[212]

Today, Guyana still views the results of that 1899 arbitration as binding. Venezuela, though, has held a revisionist view on the matter since the 1960s, and believes the 1899 decision to be null and void. Until recently, however, this has remained largely an abstract position. But in the mid-2010s, Essequibo was the site of a significant offshore energy discovery, making it the focus of intense geoeconomic interest – and whetting Venezuela's appetite to revise the prevailing *status quo.*

To that end, the Maduro regime staged a popular referendum on the subject in late 2023. The results provided a resounding mandate for action,

---

211   See, for instance, "Iran's Raisi secures array of agreements on Latin American tour," *Al-Jazeera,* June 16, 2023, https://www.aljazeera.com/news/2023/6/16/iran-president-secures-array-of-agreements-on-latin-american-tour.

212   "Award regarding the Boundary between the Colony of British Guiana and the United States of Venezuela," in United Nations, *Reports of International Tribunal Awards* XXVIII, October 3, 1899, 331-340, https://legal.un.org/riaa/cases/vol_XXVIII/331-340.pdf.

with more than 95 percent of those polled approving the establishment of a new Venezuelan state there.[213] In its wake, Maduro has made concrete moves to exercise sovereignty over the area, including mobilizing the national military, drafting an official map incorporating Essequibo into Venezuela's national boundaries, and appointing a governor for the yet-to-be-established region.[214] Informed experts now believe that, unless thwarted, concrete military moves by the Maduro regime to assert its sovereignty over the Essequibo are only a matter of time.[215]

---

213 See, for example, Vanessa Buschluter, "Essequibo: Venezuelans back claim to Guyana-controlled oil region," *BBC*, December 4, 2023, https://www.bbc.com/news/world-latin-america-67610200.

214 Floriantonia Singer, "Venezuela-Guyana dispute: Maduro mobilizes the army and announces annexation of Essequibo," *El Pais*, December 6, 2023, https://english.elpais.com/international/2023-12-06/venezuela-guyana-dispute-maduro-mobilizes-the-army-and-announces-annexation-of-essequibo.html.

215 Author's conversations, Fall 2024.

Modes of Cooperation

Over the past decade, the parallel imperial pursuits of China, Russia and Iran have propelled the three countries into increasingly close alignment. Today, cooperation among them spans multiple domains, and represents a major facet of the respective foreign policies of each. While an exhaustive detailing of the intricacies of these relationships lies beyond the scope of this work, tracing the evolution of these relationships is useful in illustrating how today's new imperialists established their partnerships – and what, precisely, these alliances currently entail.

China-Russia: Evolution Of The "No Limits" Partnership

Relations between Russia and China stretch back centuries, shifting with the priorities of the successive empires that ruled each. For much of that time, however, they were generally adversarial, as the two jockeyed for geo-political position and valuable strategic territory. Thus, China's defeat of Russian forces in 17th century clashes over the Amur River valley led to the 1689 Treaty of Nerchinsk, which recognized Chinese sovereignty over what is now the Russian Far East as well as much of present-day Eastern Siberia. But a China weakened by the Second Opium War subsequently lost that land to Russia in the late 19th Century.

During the Cold War, the initial ideological affinity that prevailed between the USSR and the PRC following the latter's 1953 establishment quickly gave way to suspicion and competition, culminating in the Sino-

Soviet split of 1961. Thereafter, the two countries engaged in a pitched ideological contest for control over the direction and composition of the international communist movement.[216] This period of tensions – which even included a brief military skirmish in 1969 over Damansky Island in the Russian Far East, opposite Manchuria[217] – began to recede following the 1976 death of the PRC's first chairman, Mao Zedong. But ties remained limited, with the two nations continuing to eye each other with suspicion until the USSR's demise.

Following the Cold War, however, China and the Soviet Union's successor, the Russian Federation, gradually began to drift closer together. The 1990s saw a series of tentative confidence-building measures between Moscow and Beijing, as well as the shared embrace of "multipolarity" as a means to balance the post-Cold War geopolitical dominance of the United States.[218] That trendline accelerated over time, as the new Russian government progressively turned away from partnership with the West in favor of an independent foreign policy orientation.[219] It culminated in the 2001 Sino-Russian Treaty of Friendship and Good Neighborliness, which was signed by Russian President Vladimir Putin and then-Chinese President Jiang Zemin in July of that year. The pact codified a new era of cooperation between the two countries, enshrining extensive economic cooperation, establishing permanent political channels and collaboration in multinational forums, and shaping a joint approach to security affairs.[220] Significant, too, was the Treaty's demarcation of territorial boundaries between Russia and China in the Far East – something that had remained a bone of contention between Moscow and Beijing in decades past.

Other signs of strategic alignment also became evident during this

---

216 This contest is extensively detailed in Lorenz M. Luthi, *The Sino-Soviet Split: Cold War in the Communist World* (Princeton University Press, 2008).

217 For an exhaustive account of that conflict, see Harrison E. Salisbury, *War Between Russia and China* (W.W. Norton, 1969).

218 See, for instance, Huiyun Feng, "Partnering Up in the New Cold War? Explaining China-Russia Relations in the Post-Cold War Era," in Brandon K. Yoder, ed., *The United States and Contemporary China-Russia Relations* (Palgrave-MacMillan, 2022).

219 An excellent summary of this changing trajectory can be found in Andrei Kozyrev, *Firebird: The Elusive Fate of Russian Democracy* (University of Pittsburgh Press, 2019).

220 Ministry of Foreign Affairs, People's Republic of China, *Treaty of Good-Neighborliness and Friendly Cooperation Between the People's Republic of China and the Russian Federation*, July 24, 2001, https://www.mfa.gov.cn/eng/zy/gb/202405/t20240531_11367098.html.

period. That same year, Russia became a charter member of the Shanghai Cooperation Organization, assuming a leadership role in the Beijing-led Eurasian political, economic and security alliance that served as the successor to the so-called "Shanghai Five." Since then, Russia and China have jointly steered the regional bloc to significant prominence. The subsequent decade also saw increased Sino-Russian cooperation on a range of issues, from military exercises to energy deals, as the two countries broadened bilateral contacts and leaned into the benefits of strategic alignment.

Russia's 2014 invasion of Ukraine deepened the partnership further still. In the aftermath of Moscow's unilateral annexation of the Crimean Peninsula, the two sides concluded a 30-year natural gas supply deal, laying the groundwork for future pipeline projects – and began to align their respective foreign policy projects: the BRI for China, and the Eurasian Economic Union for Russia.[221] Subsequently, in 2019, the two countries upgraded their relationship to a "Comprehensive Strategic Partnership," signaling a shared commitment to multi-domain coordination spanning the economic, military and political spheres.

Ultimately, in February of 2002, Presidents Putin and Xi publicly announced the creation of a "no limits" partnership between their respective regimes. The move was fraught with symbolism. As observers noted at the time, the declaration was tantamount to a "pledge to stand shoulder to shoulder against America and the West, ideologically as well as militarily."[222]

The most important stress test of these "no limits" bonds has unquestionably been Ukraine. On the heels of the joint statement, the Kremlin launched its full-scale invasion of its western neighbor. China, despite its avowed support for the principles of state sovereignty and non-interference, did not condemn Russia's decision, and has consistently abstained from international measures censuring the Kremlin. To the contrary, the PRC

221 Alexei Anishchuk, "As Putin looks east, China and Russia sign $400-billion gas deal," Reuters, May 21, 2014, https://www.reuters.com/article/business/as-putin-looks-east-china-and-russia-sign-400-billion-gas-deal-idUSBREA4K07L/; Oleg Remyga, "Linking the Eurasian Economic Union and China's Belt and Road," CSIS Reconnecting Asia, November 9, 2018, https://reconasia.csis.org/linking-eurasian-economic-union-and-chinas-belt-and-road/.

222 Robin Wright, "Russia and China Unveil Pact Against America and the West," New Yorker, February 7, 2022, https://www.newyorker.com/news/daily-comment/russia-and-china-unveil-a-pact-against-america-and-the-west.

has become a critical pillar of Russia's war effort. It has supplied the Russian military with crucial dual-use technology and military-technical support, including navigation equipment, components for fighter aircraft, and electronic warfare systems.[223] Operating via third countries, Chinese firms have shipped rifles, body armor and drone components to equip Russian forces.[224] And it has circumvented sanctions levied by the West to provide Moscow with sensors, microchips and machine tools.[225]

In the process, Beijing has become a critical enabler of the Kremlin's ongoing war of aggression – and has helped materially to perpetuate it. In his April 2025 testimony before the Senate Armed Services Committee, Admiral Samuel Parparo, the commander of U.S. Indo-Pacific Command, outlined that China has provided 70% of the machine tools and 90% of the legacy chips to Russia, thereby allowing the Kremlin to "rebuild its war machine" after unexpected early battlefield losses.[226]

China-Iran: A New Alignment

Political and economic contacts between China and Iran stretch back centuries, thanks to the fabled Silk Road of antiquity, which created trade links between east and west. Until quite recently, however, contemporary Sino-Iranian relations remained constrained because of the PRC's limited interest in the Middle East. As recently as the 2000s, scholars have documented, Beijing viewed the region primarily through two limited lenses: arms and energy. The first reflected the region's attractiveness as a lucrative market for China's weapons producers.[227] The second was generated by the demands of

223 A detailed accounting can be found in the ODNI's July 2023 report on "Support Provided by the People's Republic of China to Russia." An unclassified version of the report is available at https://democrats-intelligence.house.gov/uploadedfiles/odni_report_on_chinese_support_to_russia.pdf.

224 Erin Banco and Sarah Anne Aarup, "'Hunting rifles' – really? China ships assault weapons and body armor to Russia," *Politico*, March 16, 2023, https://www.politico.com/news/2023/03/16/chinese-rifles-body-armor-russia-ukraine-00087398.

225 See, for instance, Tom Porter, "Ukraine has accused China of supplying key equipment and supplies to Russian defense manufacturing facilities," *Business Insider*, May 28, 2025, https://www.businessinsider.com/ukraine-official-says-china-supplying-russia-military-production-factories-weapons-2025-5.

226 Lolita C. Baldor, "China, North Korea and Russia military cooperation raises threats in the Pacific, US official warns," Associated Press, April 10, 2025, https://apnews.com/article/pacific-russia-china-north-korea-weapons-ukraine-8ad7156898f1391557d5e53d5d09a02c.

227 Dan Blumenthal, "China and the Middle East: Providing Arms," *Middle East Quarterly*, Spring 2005, 11-19.

the PRC's own significant, sustained economic growth, and by a deficit of domestic sources of energy by which to fuel it.[228]

Notably, however, the early seeds of China's contemporary cooperation with Iran were sown during this period. In the 1990s, Chinese transfers of missile boats and other naval assets were essential to Iran's efforts to bolster its maritime warfare capabilities.[229] Thereafter, a Chinese commitment to pare back defense contacts with Iran in response to Western pressure led to a temporary slackening of defense sales, but saw Iran leverage technology provided by the PRC to continue to augment its capabilities.[230]

Nevertheless, contacts continued – albeit in different form. China, for instance, played a historic role in helping to stabilize the Iranian regime's hold on power. In 2009, the controversial reelection of Mahmoud Ahmadinejad to the Iranian presidency led to the rise of the Green Movement, a mass uprising that sought to affect significant "behavioral change" on the part of the ruling regime in Tehran. The accompanying mobilization relied heavily on the use of the internet to coordinate, organize and strategize. In response, the Iranian regime rapidly accelerated its presence in – and control of – the internet domain. It did so with assistance. Chinese companies such as ZTE played a key role in enhancing the Iranian regime's digital control and surveillance capabilities, allowing authorities to better track and ultimately to throttle the Green Movement.[231] (Since then, Chinese firms have remained a key part of the Iranian regime's domestic apparatus for digital repression, including playing a prominent role in the regime's evolving National Information Network.[232])

The launch of China's Belt & Road Initiative in 2013 elevated the Islamic Republic's importance in Beijing's eyes. Iran's strategic location atop the Strait of Hormuz made it a vital maritime and energy hub, while its posi-

---

228 Jin Liangxiang, "China and the Middle East: Energy First," *Middle East Quarterly*, Spring 2005, 3-10.

229 https://www.uscc.gov/sites/default/files/Research/China-Iran--A%20Limited%20Partnership.pdf.

230 Ibid.

231 See, for instance, Steve Stecklow, "Special Report: Chinese firm helps Iran spy on citizens," Reuters, March 22, 2012, https://www.reuters.com/article/world/special-report-chinese-firm-helps-iran-spy-on-citizens-idUSBRE82L0BC/.

232 See Calla O'Neil, "Iran's Digital Fortress: The Rise of the National Information Network," American Foreign Policy Council *Iran Strategy Brief* no. 16, August 2025, https://www.afpc.org/uploads/documents/Iran_Strategy_Brief_No._16_-_August_2025.pdf.

tion between Central Asia and the Persian Gulf created a vital corridor for Chinese commerce with Europe and the Middle East. Accordingly, the PRC invested deeply in Iran's infrastructure, financing projects like the Tehran-Mashhad electrification project and helping to bankroll rail links between the Islamic Republic and Central Asian states such as Turkmenistan.[233] Over the years, China has also invested in the development of assorted Iranian oil fields as part of a deepening energy stake in the Islamic Republic.[234]

Iran's attractiveness in this regard is driven by China's own economic circumstances. Over the past fifteen years, Chinese energy consumption has soared, propelled by what until comparatively recently has been robust economic growth. China, however, lacks sufficient domestic sources of energy, and as a result has been forced to rely more and more heavily on foreign sources of oil, the Middle East prominent among them. The region is estimated to provide a significant percentage of China's imports of crude oil (40% of more),[235] while Iran makes up a notable portion of this total: nearly 14%.[236] All of which has helped make Iran an attractive energy destination for the PRC. This energy partnership, in turn, has been facilitated by lackluster American policy. While U.S. sanctions constrained China's energy trade with Iran between 2018 and 2020, Iran's total energy exports have ballooned over the past half-decade – and last year were estimated to average some 1.5 million barrels per day.[237] Continued access to this energy flow represents a cardinal imperative for China's leadership, which has taken great pains to ensure it.

That has involved drawing the Islamic Republic ever closer and positioning itself as a key guarantor of stability for Iran's clerical regime. Thus,

233 "Tehran-Mashhad electrification loan signed," *Railway Gazette International*, July 25, 2017, https://www.railwaygazette.com/infrastructure/tehran-mashhad-electrification-loan-signed/44900.article; "China and Iran agree on massive electrification project," railfreight.com, July 21, 2025, https://www.railfreight.com/beltandroad/2025/07/21/china-and-iran-agree-on-massive-electrification-project/.

234 Laurie Chen and Ethan Wang, "What are China's economic interests in Iran?" Reuters, June 24, 2025, https://www.reuters.com/world/middle-east/what-are-chinas-economic-interests-iran-2025-06-24/.

235 Detailed in U.S.-China Economic and Security Review Commission, *2024 Annual Report to Congress*, November 2024, https://www.uscc.gov/sites/default/files/2024-11/Chapter_5--China_and_the_Middle_East.pdf.

236 "China's heavy reliance on Iranian oil imports," Reuters, June 24, 2025, https://www.reuters.com/business/energy/chinas-heavy-reliance-iranian-oil-imports-2025-06-24/.

237 U.S. Department of Energy, Energy Information Administration, "Country Analysis Brief: Iran," October 10, 2024, https://www.eia.gov/international/content/analysis/countries_long/Iran/pdf/Iran%20CAB%202024.pdf.

in the Spring of 2020, the two countries signed a sprawling, 25-year, $400 billion strategic cooperation agreement encompassing sectors such as energy, infrastructure and telecommunications. For Iran, the decision to deepen ties with China were, at least in part, a reaction to the Trump administration's "maximum pressure" campaign, which had precipitated a collapse of its national currency and severely curtailed its energy exports.[238] For China, meanwhile, the arrangement provided the PRC with "first mover advantage" in the Iranian economy, as well as giving it preferential access to new ports (and potentially naval bases). While experts say that the vast majority of these provisions remain notional,[239] the deal lays the groundwork for a further expansion of the already-extensive alignment between the two countries in the years ahead, as China continues to expand its influence in – and leverage over – the Middle East.

Russia-Iran: From Marriage of Convenience to Strategic Union

Today's diplomatic contacts between Tehran and Moscow can be traced back to the Ayatollah Ruhollah Khomeini's 1979 Revolution, which transformed the previously pro Western country into an enemy of the United States and a potential partner for the USSR. But the contemporary relationship between the two countries did not emerge until after the Soviet collapse. When it did, it was because of both practical and ideological reasons.

The breakup of the USSR had unleashed a host of new problems for Russia, significant among them the rise of ethnic and religious separatism in the majority-Muslim republics of Central Asia. The Kremlin was eager to mitigate the threat that these forces posed to social cohesion and political order in its "near abroad," and to stave off their potential destabilizing impact within its own borders. Here, the Islamic Republic loomed large as

---

238   Ilan Berman, "What Iran Gets from the Strategic Deal with China," New Lines Institute, July 29, 2020, https://newlinesinstitute.org/strategic-competition/china/what-iran-gets-from-the-strategic-deal-with-china/.

239   See, for instance, Laurie Chen and Ethan Wang, "What are China's economic interests in Iran?" Reuters, June 24, 2025, https://www.reuters.com/world/middle-east/what-are-chinas-economic-interests-iran-2025-06-24/.

a potential problem, because of its well-established pedigree of "exporting the revolution," a practice which had caused tremendous instability in the Middle East in the preceding decade. Moscow was justifiably fearful that, given the nascent connections between Iran and the Central Asian states, Tehran could end up playing a similar, destabilizing role there as well unless it was properly engaged.

That imperative intersected with the country's commercial imperatives. In the early 1990s, Russia's defense industry was in shambles, hit hard by the Soviet collapse. Russian officials were therefore hungry for new clients that could put it back on firm footing, and Iran fit this bill. The Islamic Republic's eight-year war with neighboring Iraq (1980-1988) had left its military decimated and in dire need of new infusions of military material. Meanwhile, Iranian officials saw a natural role for their country in the new, anti-Western foreign policy being promulgated by then-Russian Prime Minister Yevgeny Primakov.[240] The result was a meeting of the minds in which the Islamic Republic become a major recipient of Russian arms in exchange for its commitment to eschew meddling on the territory of the former Soviet Union.

Quickly, however, the arrangement blossomed into something more – a long-term union aimed at diluting the power and dominance of the U.S. (and thereby its allies, such as Israel) in global affairs. As part of that evolution, Russia became a key enabler of Iran's nuclear ambitions, constructing and subsequently administering the reactor in the Iranian port city of Bushehr. It also championed diplomatic arrangements, such as the 2015 nuclear deal known as the Joint Comprehensive Plan of Action, that protect and enshrine the regime's nuclear effort. Likewise, the Kremlin became an advocate for Iran in assorted diplomatic forums, using its permanent seat on the UN Security Council to consistently dilute multilateral sanctions levied on the Iranian regime for its nuclear drive and its persistent support of terrorism. Russia also has worked to integrate the Islamic Republic into non-Western blocs, ranging from the Shanghai Cooperation Organization

---

240   Ariel Cohen, "The 'Primakov Doctrine': Russia's Zero Sum Game with the United States," Heritage Foundation *F.Y.I.* no. 167, December 15, 1997, https://www.heritage.org/report/the-primakov-doctrine-russias-zero-sum-game-the-united-states.

to the BRICS economic grouping, thereby bolstering the Islamic Republic's physical and economic security. When Iran's financial institutions were disconnected from the SWIFT international banking system (initially in 2012, and then again in 2018), Russian entities built banking arrangements that allowed the country to continue to carry out international commerce. Moscow likewise has bankrolled extensive transport links (such as the Rasht-Astana railway) that have helped Iran to integrate more deeply into regional economic arrangements in the "post-Soviet space." And it erected extensive partnerships with the Islamic Republic in the fields of oil and natural gas, thereby facilitating large scale energy swaps that diluted the effectiveness of the international sanctions being levied by the United States and other Western powers.

Notably, this support has long been more than simply practical. The Islamic Republic has been viewed by the country's neo-imperialist thinkers as a natural ally and integral part of the "Eurasian axis" that Moscow needs to erect on its road back to global greatness. Thus, in his magnum opus, *Osnovy Geopolitiki* [The Foundations of Geopolitics], far-right ideologue Alexander Dugin argued that:

...Iran occupies such a position on the map of the continent that the creation of a Moscow-Tehran axis solves a great number of problems facing the New Empire [Russia]. By including Iran as the Western pole of the Empire, Russia would immediately achieve the strategic goal which it has sought (through incorrect paths) for several hundred years: access to warm seas.[241]

Nevertheless, it would be fair to say that the historic partnership between Russia and Iran has been deeply unequal. For much of the time that Moscow has allied itself with Tehran, it has clearly served as the "senior partner" in the relationship. Not so now, however. Russia's full-scale invasion of Ukraine in February 2022, and the persistent campaign of aggression

---

241   Alexander Dugin, *Osnovy Geopolitiki: Geopoliticheskoye Budushiye Rossiyi* [The Foundations of Geopolitics: Russia's Geopolitical Future] (Arktogaia-center, 2000), 241. (Author's translation)

that has been waged by the Kremlin since, has opened a new page in the Russo-Iranian strategic partnership. It has also helped turn the traditional dynamics of the strategic alliance between the two countries on their head. Unforeseen battlefield difficulties, and sustained Western support for Kyiv, have forced Russia to progressively turn to external allies to both backstop and augment its military campaign.

Iran has played an important role in this regard. The Islamic Republic has emerged as a significant source of weaponry and war material for the Kremlin. These war supplies have included short-range ballistic missiles, as well as large quantities of artillery and small arms ammunition and the logistics to move them.[242] The centerpiece of Iranian support, however, has been the provision of unmanned aerial vehicles to augment the Russian war effort. Beginning in the Fall of 2023, Iran's regime committed to the provision of advanced *Shahed* attack drones to Russia, supplying the Kremlin with hundreds of drone platforms that were used against Ukraine as well as modified for improved performance.[243] The following year saw the expansion of this partnership via the creation, by Russia, of a specialized industrial zone in its republic of Tatarstan to commence the local production of thousands of Iranian-designed drones.[244] The cumulative effect has been nothing short of transformative for Russia's war effort.

The Islamic Republic has benefited handsomely as a result. In her March 2025 testimony before the Senate Select Committee on Intelligence, Director of National Intelligence Tulsi Gabbard noted: "Iran has become a critical military supplier to Russia, especially of UAVs, in exchange for Russian technical support for Iranian weapons, intelligence, and advanced cyber capabilities."[245] And more is assuredly to come. In April of 2025,

---

242 See, for instance, Hanna Notte and Jim Lamson, "Iran-Russia Defense Cooperation: Current Realities and Future Horizons," Middlebury Institute of International Studies at Monterey, *CNS Occasional Paper* no. 61, August 2024, https://nonproliferation.org/wp-content/uploads/2024/08/op61-RSI_Russia-Iran_Notte-Lamson_CNS-Occasional-Paper.pdf.

243 Tuqa Khalid, "Moscow enhancing Iran-made Shahed drones with Russian weapons modifications: UK," *Al Arabiya*, December 6, 2023, https://english.alarabiya.net/News/world/2023/12/07/Moscow-enhancing-Iran-made-Shahed-drones-with-Russian-weapons-modifications-UK.

244 Benoit Faucon, Nicholas Bariyo and Matthew Luxmoore, "The Russian Drone Plant That Could Shape the War in Ukraine," *Wall Street Journal*, May 28, 2024, https://www.wsj.com/world/the-russian-drone-plant-that-could-shape-the-war-in-ukraine-7abd5616.

245 Tulsi Gabbard, Statement before the Senate Select Committee on Intelligence, March 25, 2025, https://www.dni.gov/files/ODNI/documents/assessments/ATA-2025-Testimony-As-Prepared.pdf.

the Duma, Russia's lower house of parliament, ratified a new, two-decade strategic partnership agreement with the Islamic Republic. That pact, which had been hammered out by Russian President Vladimir Putin and Iranian President Masoud Pezeshkian, expands cooperation between the two countries on military and security issues, and contains a framework for stepped-up joint military drills, both on Russian and Iranian territory and potentially beyond.[246]

Trilateral Convergence

In recent years, much to the alarm of policymakers in the West, these bilateral partnerships have drifted closer together, as cooperation among China, Russia and Iran has expanded into extensive triangulation across a range of activities.

For instance, the three countries have established a regular schedule of military contacts, drills and exercises. Since 2019, annual trilateral naval maneuvers in and around the waters of the Gulf of Oman, officially dubbed Marine/Maritime Security Belt, have strengthened coordination among the three in things like maritime interdiction and anti-piracy operations.[247] These exercises have been coupled with a ministerial-level defense dialogue – the most recent of which took place on the sidelines of the June 2025 SCO summit in Qingdao, China.[248] Iran has likewise been welcomed as a full-fledged member of that grouping, which Iranian officials hope will expand over time to provide collective security protections and guarantees that would strengthen its own security.

Economically, trade between the three countries also has ballooned in recent years, as their political proximity opened the door for increased com-

246 "Russia's lower house of parliament ratifies 20-year pact between Russia and Iran," Reuters, April 8, 2025, https://www.reuters.com/world/europe/russian-lower-house-parliament-ratifies-20-year-pact-between-russia-iran-2025-04-08/.

247 U.S. Department of Defense, *Annual Report to Congress: Military and Security Developments Involving the People's Republic of China 2024*, 2025, https://media.defense.gov/2024/Dec/18/2003615520/-1/-1/0/MILITARY-AND-SECURITY-DEVELOPMENTS-INVOLVING-THE-PEOPLES-REPUBLIC-OF-CHINA-2024.PDF.

248 "China hosts Iranian, Russian defence ministers against backdrop of 'momentous change,'" Agence France-Presse, June 26, 2025, https://hongkongfp.com/2025/06/26/china-hosts-iranian-russian-defence-ministers-against-backdrop-of-momentous-change/.

merce. Between Russia and China, for instance, bilateral trade has expanded in parallel with warming ties – and surged since the start of the Ukraine war, as Western markets progressively shut their doors to Russian goods. In 2024, Sino-Russian trade stood at $245 billion annually, more than double the figure tallied in 2020.[249] Trade between Russia and Iran has followed a similar trajectory; following a significant decline in the 2010s as a result of Western sanctions, it has grown from just over $1 billion annually in 2020 to nearly $5 billion in 2024.[250] As for Sino-Iranian trade, while it has declined notably over the past decade as a result of renewed sanctions (now tallied at some $13.4 billion[251]), China's deep dependence on Iranian oil has sustained economic ties – and deepened Beijing's reliance on the Islamic Republic. Reuters reports that, as of June 2025, nearly 90% of Iranian oil exports were going to China, an average of 1.38 million barrels daily.[252]

The three countries have likewise aligned their monetary policies. Russia and China, for instance, have collaborated on "de-dollarization" over the past several years as a way of sanctions-proofing their respective economies, with an increasing percentage of their bilateral trade now conducted in the Chinese *yuan* as a consequence.[253] Iran is likewise interested in reducing its dependence on the U.S. dollar, thereby blunting the impact of continuing American sanctions – a posture that aligns it with Beijing's efforts to internationalize its currency.[254] Predictably, all three countries have encouraged the BRICS economic grouping first to carry out trade in the local currencies of its members, and subsequently backed an independent

249 "China-Russia Dashboard: a special relationship in facts and figures," Mercator Institute for China Studies, n.d., https://merics.org/en/china-russia-dashboard-facts-and-figures-special-relationship.

250 "Iran and Russia: Gyrating Trade Grows," United States Institute of Peace *Iran Primer*, May 18, 2023, https://iranprimer.usip.org/blog/2023/may/18/iran-and-russia-gyrating-trade-grows; "Russia-Iran trade turnover grows by 16.2% in 2024 to $4.8 billion – energy minister," TASS, April 25, 2025, https://tass.com/economy/1949413.

251 "China imports from Iran," Trading Economics, n.d., https://tradingeconomics.com/china/imports/iran; "China exports to Iran," Trading Economics, n.d., https://tradingeconomics.com/china/exports/iran.

252 "China's heavy reliance on Iranian oil imports," Reuters, June 24, 2025, https://www.reuters.com/business/energy/chinas-heavy-reliance-iranian-oil-imports-2025-06-24/.

253 See, for instance, Maia Nikoladze and Mrugank Bhusari, "Russia and China have been teaming up to reduce reliance on the dollar. Here's how it's going," *New Atlanticist*, February 22, 2023, https://www.atlanticcouncil.org/blogs/new-atlanticist/russia-and-china-have-been-teaming-up-to-reduce-reliance-on-the-dollar-heres-how-its-going/.

254 Tom Wilson, "The Iranian connection: how China is importing oil from Russia," *Financial Times*, August 20, 2025, https://www.ft.com/content/19cebbc7-c6d7-4050-b80c-0b9f8d334d7a.

currency for the bloc, known as "BRICS pay." While ostensibly a tool to facilitate commerce, it is abundantly clear that "BRICS pay" will serve a geopolitical purpose as well. Russian Foreign Minister Sergei Lavrov signaled as much when he told an international symposium in November of 2024 that such alternative currencies are needed because "The dollar, long touted as the global commons of humanity, has been weaponised to suppress and penalise geopolitical competitors and the non-compliant."[255]

In the disinformation and propaganda space, meanwhile, recent years has seen a notable convergence among Moscow, Beijing and Tehran. All three countries have, when opportune for them to do so, amplified each other's narratives on a range of issues – with the shared goal of tarnishing America's image as a global leader. [256] This was particularly noticeable over the course of the COVID-19 pandemic, when experts saw significant "narrative alignment" between Russian, Chinese and Iranian media sources. The state-controlled messaging organs of all three countries parroted the same conspiracy theories and misinformation, including that the disease was an American bioweapon.[257] So robust was this partnership that some analysts termed it an "axis of disinformation."[258]

This activity, moreover, has continued well beyond the pandemic. In its September 2024 study on disinformation, the U.S. Government Accountability Office identified China, Russia and Iran as "the main foreign governments that have been creating and spreading disinformation..."[259] And multiple assessments in 2024 and 2025, from institutions as varied as the U.S. Office of the Director of National Intelligence, the North Atlantic

---

255 Sergei Lavrov, Remarks at the International Symposium on "Investing in the Future," Moscow, Russia, November 4, 2024, https://www.mid.ru/en/foreign_policy/rso/asean/1979085/?TSPD_101_R0=08765fb817ab2000fc8df736bfcadc571f635db7917c0ca-ac12508cedc9d691e54a8dcf56c55f57a08e002a5771430002a032c3f9fd50988642459a7d-1b580809672e485eb3648cf4fc0bdda852d531d3ab01769f7d72c0cf6761df37fd7a2b6.

256 Clint Watts, "Triad of Disinformation: How Russia, Iran, & China Ally in a Messaging War Against America," German Marshall Fund *Alliance for Securing Democracy*, May 15, 2020, https://securingdemocracy.gmfus.org/triad-of-disinformation-how-russia-iran-china-ally-in-a-messaging-war-against-america/.

257 Ibid.

258 Andrew Whiskeyman and Michael Berger, "Axis of Disinformation: Propaganda from Iran, Russia, and China on COVID-19," Washington Institute for Near East Policy *Fikra Forum*, February 28, 2021, https://www.washingtoninstitute.org/policy-analysis/axis-disinformation-propaganda-iran-russia-and-china-covid-19.

259 U.S. Government Accountability Office, "FOREIGN DISINFORMATION: Defining and Detecting Threats," GAO-24-107600, September 26, 2024, https://www.gao.gov/assets/gao-24-107600.pdf.

Treaty Organization, and the Microsoft Corporation have found growing alignment among Beijing, Moscow and Tehran in the goals, narratives and methods of their disinformation efforts – including "cross-amplification" and the growing use of artificial intelligence to boost the effectiveness and reach of their propaganda.[260] The objectives of these efforts are shared: to erode trust in democratic institutions, to sow division in Western societies, and to diminish the standing of the United States and other countries on the world stage.

Notably, all three appear likewise to be sharing "best practices" relating to domestic digital control and censorship. As recent reports have noted, the authoritarian models now being promulgated by Beijing, Moscow and Tehran in how to surveil and control their respective populations, as well as safeguard the country from Western influence and unwelcome news, closely resemble one another in objectives – even if the particulars of these efforts differ.[261]

Chinese, Russian and Iranian cooperation, in other words, is increasingly becoming a trilateral affair. Today, all three countries are seeking to harness the benefits of their existing bilateral partnership and harness them as part of an expanded alliance. They are doing so to advance shared imperial appetites, and to subvert a Western-led order that stands in the way of those desires.

---

260 Gabbard, Statement before the Senate Select Committee on Intelligence, March 25, 2025; Jerker Hellstrom, Matti Puranen, Santeri Kytoneva and Pekka Kallioniemi, "Are Russian Narratives Amplified by PRC Media?" North Atlantic Treaty Organization Strategic Communications Center of Excellence, February 2024; https://stratcomcoe.org/publications/download/Russian-Narratives-PRC-Media-DIGITAL.pdf; Clint Watts, "As the U.S. election nears, Russia, Iran and China step up influence efforts," Microsoft Corporation, October 23, 2024, https://blogs.microsoft.com/on-the-issues/2024/10/23/as-the-u-s-election-nears-russia-iran-and-china-step-up-influence-efforts/.

261 O'Neil, "Iran's Digital Fortress: The Rise of the National Information Network."

Confronting The New Imperialists

How might the United States best respond to the combined threat posed by today's new imperialists? For policymakers in Washington, addressing the challenge posed by the ambitions of China, Russia and Iran – and by the growing interplay now taking place between them – requires properly understanding and applying strategies that activate allies, leverage the seams between America's adversaries, and address their ambitions. That conversation, in turn, begins with deterrence.

The Dynamics of Deterrence

After decades of Cold War geopolitics, the contemporary scholarship on deterrence – what works, what doesn't, and what matters in shaping the behavior of one's adversaries – is positively voluminous. Our goal here is not to recycle the works of strategic thinkers like Thomas Shelling or Colin Gray. Rather, it is to distill a number of key lessons learned about the nature of deterrence that are germane to the strategic environment currently confronting the United States.

The first is that deterrence is not a static condition. Rather, it is part of a dynamic interaction between adversaries, as well as a psychological assessment by both. Nations contemplating aggression do not simply measure the number of tanks, ships, or aircraft arrayed against them (although they assuredly take those into account). They also weigh whether the defender has the will to use them, whether its political leadership is prepared to sustain a fight, and if the country in question possesses the social cohesion required to endure the inevitable costs and hardships of conflict. This duality – capability and will – helps to explain why deterrence succeeds at times and fails at others.

The United States today faces the most complex deterrence challenge since the Cold War. Three revisionist powers are now actively probing for weaknesses in the international system and the existing rules-based order. As the bipartisan Congressional Commission on National Defense Strategy bluntly outlined in its 2024 final report: "The United States faces the most challenging global environment with the most severe ramifications since the end of the Cold War. The trends are getting worse, not better."[262]

Each of today's strategic adversaries, in turn, is motivated by a blend of historical grievance, ideological ambition, and opportunism. And each is calibrating its behavior not only to America's material strength, but also to its political steadfastness.

Therein lies America's current challenge. The ability to deter aggression, or to compel adversaries to back down, depends not only on raw military strength but on whether that power is believed to be usable and sustainable. America's deterrent posture is strengthened when allies act in concert, when military-industrial systems are agile, and when adversaries are uncertain about U.S. redlines. It weakens when bureaucratic inertia, fractured alliances, or domestic political dysfunction call American resolve into question – as they do today.

The State of American Alliances

The second is that, increasingly, the United States is not in a position to shoulder this burden alone. As the Commission notes, the Pentagon operates at "the speed of bureaucracy" while threats approach "wartime urgency." Additionally, current force-sizing models are inadequate for confronting simultaneous challenges in Europe, the Indo-Pacific, and the Middle East.

---

262   *Report of the Commission on the National Defense Strategy* (Santa Monica: RAND, July 2024), https://www.armed-services.senate.gov/imo/media/doc/nds_commission_final_report.pdf.

And U.S. defense industrial production is alarmingly insufficient, incapable of generating the munitions, systems, and technologies needed to sustain prolonged conflict, let alone surge for great power war.[263]

These deficiencies are not lost on America's adversaries. Beijing sees a U.S. military stretched thin and doubts Washington's ability to fight simultaneously in Europe, the Middle East, and the Indo-Pacific. Moscow has calculated that Western industrial capacity cannot sustain Ukraine indefinitely. Tehran, meanwhile, continues to test U.S. resolve through proxies, and remains confident that Washington fears protracted escalation.

Here, America's extended network of alliances should, in principle, provide a much-needed backstop. After all, alliances – whether the Allied Powers of World War II, the Western "sphere of influence" during the Cold War, or the "coalitions of the willing" of the post 9/11 era – have always served as America's greatest asymmetric advantage. They extend reach, multiply power, and bind together coalitions of democracies in ways that authoritarian adversaries cannot easily match. Yet a closer inspection reveals that, in the relevant theaters, the U.S. alliance structure remains deeply deficient.

Thus Europe, for all its bluster and current activism in response to both U.S. pressure and Russian predation, remains militarily and industrially fragile – vulnerabilities that have the potential to embolden adversaries. (And which, in the case of Russia, already have). Part of that is undoubtedly a consequence of history. European military capability was always meant to complement, rather than replicate, American power. The architecture of NATO assumes that U.S. forces would bear the brunt of any major continental conflict, with European armies playing a supplemental role. As a result, many European states allowed their forces to atrophy during the post–Cold War period.

That neglect now shows in a number of ways.

The lion's share of **NATO**'s 3.5 million military personnel is provided by the United States (about 1.3 million) and Turkey (500,000 between active-duty troops and gendarmerie). Of NATO's 30 remaining members,

---

263   Ibid.

only six have armies exceeding 100,000 troops. The other two dozen collectively contribute about 750,000 soldiers—most with limited expeditionary capabilities or high degrees of readiness.

Britain, historically one of NATO's heavyweights, now finds itself stretched perilously thin. Its military is now at its smallest size in over two centuries, and Lord Dannatt, the former head of the British Army, has warned that the UK could scarcely sustain a 10,000-strong deployment without exhausting its capacity.[264]

With 270,000 active personnel, **France** fields Western Europe's largest force and remains one of just two nuclear powers on the continent. In recent years, it has ramped up its defense spending dramatically in response to the Russian threat.[265] Yet Paris has also retrenched from Africa, and is now able to contribute only modestly to peacekeeping in Ukraine, should it be called on to do so.[266]

Germany's grand plans for transformation – entailing growth from 180,000 soldiers to 230,000 men under arms as part of the *Zeitenwende* of former Chancellor Olaf Scholz[267] – are hamstrung by readiness woes. After significant transfers of arms to Ukraine, German forces now operate at less than 50% readiness.[268]

Other parts of the continent are even more feeble. **Italy**, a country of nearly 60 million, fields only 167,000 active-duty troops and relies on 110,000 Carabinieri, a domestic police force that can be militarized in wartime. **Spain**, meanwhile, maintains 118,000 soldiers and 80,000 members of its Civil Guard, but allocates just 1.3 percent of GDP to defense,

264 Claran McGrath, "Starmer handed chilling six-word warning by ex-army chief over UK's 'run down' military," *Express*, February 16, 2025, https://www.express.co.uk/news/world/2014897/starmer-handed-chilling-ten-word-warning.

265 Angela Charlton, "French President Macron announced 6.5 billion euros in extra military spending in next two years," Associated Press, July 13, 2025, https://apnews.com/article/france-macron-military-spending-17183f1871460e1451453a091ef6c4bd.

266 Ella Joyner, "France, UK urge 'reassurance force' for Ukraine," *Deutsche Welle*, March 27, 2025, https://www.dw.com/en/france-uk-urge-reassurance-force-for-ukraine/a-72064382.

267 Sebastian Shukla, Claudia Otto and Nadine Schmidt, "Germany is unlocking billions to supercharge its military at a seismic moment for Europe," *CNN*, March 23, 2025, https://www.cnn.com/2025/03/23/europe/germany-military-investment-intl.

268 Sabine Siebold, "'50% battle-ready': Germany misses military targets despite Scholz's overhaul," Reuters, February 13, 2025, https://www.reuters.com/world/europe/50-battle-ready-germany-misses-military-targets-despite-scholzs-overhaul-2025-02-13/.

the lowest of any NATO member, with most spent on salaries rather than modernization.[269]

Europe's industrial base paints an equally troubling picture. A 2024 study by the International Institute for Strategic Studies (IISS) concluded that, although some European countries maintain the capability to produce war material such as main battle tanks and guided munitions, their output is slow.[270] In other areas, such as rocket launchers, anti-submarine warfare platforms, and air defense systems, industrial capability has all but vanished. As a result, the continent now relies heavily on imports from the U.S., Israel, and South Korea to field those capabilities.[271]

To be sure, bright spots in this general picture do exist. In recent years, the strategic center of gravity on the European continent has shifted eastward, toward what has been called "New Europe" (countries like Poland, the Czech Republic, and the Baltic states).[272] These nations, and others on the continent's eastern flank, have had their attention focused by the proximity of a resurgent, imperial Russia. **Poland**, for instance, is now actively rearming, with over 216,000 active-duty soldiers and 50,000 territorial defense personnel and plans to raise defense spending to 5 percent of GDP even before the June 2025 NATO summit made that figure an official Alliance target.[273]

In the aggregate, however, Europe remains dangerously reliant on American leadership and material. Without deeper coordination, greater investment, and industrial consolidation, NATO's deterrent posture will remain incomplete – and adversaries will invariably take notice.

Asia's military picture, though more robust, is less cohesive. While

269 Laura Kayali and Max Griera, "Spain wants exemption from NATO's 5 percent defense spending target," *Politico*, June 19, 2025, https://www.politico.eu/article/spain-nato-summit-5-percent-defense-spending-target-perdo-sanchez-military-donald-trump/.

270 "Building Defence Capacity in Europe: An Assessment," International Institute for Strategic Studies *IISS Strategic Dossier*, 2024, https://www.iiss.org/globalassets/media-library---content--migration/files/publications---free-files/strategic-dossier/pds-2024/iiss_building-defence-capacity-in-europe-an-assessment_112024.pdf.

271 Ibid.

272 See, for instance, Jakub Knopp, "The Eastward Shift: NATO's New Centre of Gravity," Royal United Services Institute *RUSI Newsbrief*, April 25, 2023, https://www.rusi.org/explore-our-research/publications/rusi-newsbrief/eastward-shift-natos-new-centre-gravity.

273 "Poland wants to spend 5% of GDP on defence in 2026, minister says," Reuters, April 3, 2025, https://www.reuters.com/world/europe/poland-wants-spend-5-gdp-defence-2026-minister-says-2025-04-03/.

several of its states – namely Japan, South Korea, Taiwan, India, and Australia – field capable forces, the region as a whole lacks a formalized institutional framework akin to what exists in Europe. As such, the region's powers are deeply dependent on their bilateral ties to and security arrangements with Washington. Those, in turn, rely heavily on perceptions that Washington would, in fact, come to their defense if needed.

Japan, bound to the U.S. by the 1951 Treaty of Mutual Cooperation and Security, contributes $2 billion annually toward the basing of 50,000 U.S. troops on its soil. Its own Self-Defense Forces number approximately 230,000, supported by a defense budget of 1.3 percent of GDP – a figure that is now expected to rise in response to China's growing assertiveness.[274] Japan's industrial potential likewise has long been constrained by postwar restrictions. But those limitations are eroding; Tokyo's 2023–2028 "Defense Buildup Program" outlines major planned investments in domestic weapons production.[275]

South Korea, a front-line state facing North Korea's vast conventional and nuclear arsenal, spends 2.7 percent of its GDP on defense, funding a 500,000-strong military. Under a 1953 mutual defense treaty, the U.S. currently stations 24,000 troops in the ROK, reinforcing deterrence against Pyongyang and simultaneously integrating warfighting capabilities with Seoul.

India, a regional heavyweight of 1.4 billion people, boasts the world's fourth-largest defense budget. It spends roughly 2.3 percent of GDP on defense and fields an army of 1.5 million personnel. Unlike many other Asian powers, it has demonstrated a clear willingness to use force, clashing with China in the Himalayas and confronting Pakistan across multiple fronts. And in recent years, India's navy, which maintains close ties with the U.S. Navy, has taken a more active role in the Indian Ocean and South

---

274 "Panel to propose Japan weigh defense spending above 2% of GDP," *Kyodo News*, June 15, 2025, https://english.kyodonews.net/articles/-/55487?phrase=Yuzuru+&words=.

275 See, for instance, Takahashi Kosuke, "Japan Approves 9.4 Percent Increase in Defense Spending for FY2025," *The Diplomat*, December 27, 2024, https://thediplomat.com/2024/12/japan-approves-9-4-percent-increase-in-defense-spending-for-fy2025/.

China Sea, conducting joint exercises with Vietnam, Malaysia, and the Philippines.[276]

Australia, with a comparatively small population of 27 million, allocates just two percent of its GDP to maintaining a professional force of 60,000 troops. But, although modest in size, the Australian military is well-equipped and closely integrated with U.S. forces through training, intelligence sharing, and naval operations.

Even **Taiwan**, with its population of nearly 24 million, fields an active-duty force of 169,000, alongside 1.66 million reservists. That figure is growing amid mounting worries over Chinese designs over the island.[277] Under the 1979 Taiwan Relations Act, the United States is obligated to provide defensive arms and maintain a posture capable of deterring Chinese aggression. And although Taiwan is a technological leader, its ability to sustain a high-intensity military conflict depends on external resupply.

Nevertheless, doubts in the region persist among regional states regarding America's willingness to come to their aid – doubts made more acute by political disruptions and errant messaging from Washington. That uncertainty has nudged some regional states – most recently India – to seek closer partnership with the PRC as a hedge against potential hostility on its part.[278] And it has prompted several, notably South Korea, Japan, and Taiwan, to entertain the possibility of developing their own nuclear deterrents.[279]

Similarly, despite an enduring U.S. military presence, the Middle East is strategically brittle. The region lacks a formal NATO-style collective defense structure, though the closest analogue – the Gulf Cooperation Council – has shown at least some ability to mobilize forces in the face of

---

276 See, for instance, Shivani Sharma, "India's Maritime Imperative," *Newsweek*, July 26, 2024, https://www.afpc.org/publications/articles/indias-maritime-imperative.

277 Chad De Guzman, "Taiwan Is Extending Conscription. Here's How Its Military Compares to Other Countries," *TIME*, January 6, 2023, https://time.com/6245036/taiwan-conscription-military-comparison/.

278 Shanthie Mariet D'Souza, "India's China Embrace and US Decoupling," *The Diplomat*, August 30, 2025, https://thediplomat.com/2025/08/indias-china-embrace-and-us-decoupling/.

279 See, for instance, Toby Dalton, Karl Friedhoff, and Lami Kim, "Thinking Nuclear: South Korean Attitudes on Nuclear Weapons," Chicago Council on Global Affairs, February 21, 2022, https://globalaffairs.org/research/public-opinion-survey/thinking-nuclear-south-korean-attitudes-nuclear-weapons.

perceived regional threats (as it did during the "Arab Spring.") Additional early signs of other collective defense structures are also emerging.[280] For the moment, however, deterrence rests largely on an architecture of bilateral U.S. partnerships, forward basing arrangements, and *ad hoc* coalitions. This approach, though flexible, nonetheless provides gaps that adversaries (Iran foremost among them) can readily exploit.

Israel is unquestionably the region's most capable military power, with both a presumed nuclear program and a qualitative military edge undergirded by robust, ongoing American support. These capabilities have been demonstrated, in dramatic fashion, by the country's efforts since 2023 to dismantle Iran's extensive network of proxies in the region. Even so, the current post-October 7th environment has highlighted the limits of Israeli military capabilities during protracted conflicts.

Though it possesses some of the most advanced weaponry in the Gulf, thanks to large-scale, sustained arms sales by the United States and other Western powers, **Saudi Arabia**'s military effectiveness remains limited. It is hampered by inadequate training, weak command structures, and a reliance on external support from allied nations for defense.[281]

For its part, the **United Arab Emirates** boasts a small but expeditionary force with outsized influence, fielding capable air assets and special operations units.[282] However, it too is vulnerable to Iranian missile and drone strikes – a state of affairs that was driven home by the 2019 and 2022 attacks on Gulf energy infrastructure carried out by the Islamic Republic.

The kingdom of **Bahrain**, in spite of its modest size, serves as the lynchpin of U.S. maritime operations in the Gulf, hosting both the U.S. Fifth Fleet and the U.S. Naval Forces Central Command. Beyond this role,

280   Anna Ahronheim, "The Middle East Air Defense alliance takes flight," *Jerusalem Post*, July 15, 2022, https://www.jpost.com/middle-east-news/article-712150.

281   See, for instance, Yoel Guzansky and Tomer Barak, "Saudi Security: Increasing Challenges alongside Strategic Limitations," Institute for National Security Studies, August 24, 2021, https://www.inss.org.il/publication/saudi-arabia-security/#:~:text=this%20raises%20the%20question%20of,in%20particular%20in%20the%20gulf.

282   See, for instance, Michael Knights, *25 Days to Aden: The Unknown Story of Arabian Elite Forces at War* (Profile Books, 2023).

however, Bahrain fields only a modest military – some 10,000 personnel, spread between the country's Army, Air Force, Navy and Royal Guard.[283]

Despite its close present-day relations with Iran, **Qatar** plays a critical role in America's basing posture in the region. Al-Udeid air base, situated outside Doha, is currently home to some 10,000 U.S. troops, and played a critical role in American regional campaigns such as Operation Enduring Freedom (2001), Operation Iraqi Freedom (2003) and, more recently, was a principal launching point for U.S. aerial assets involved in intercepting Iranian drones and missiles fired at Israel in April 2024. The robustness of the U.S. deployment at Al-Udeid, however, masks the inherent weakness of Qatar's indigenous military capabilities, which are severely limited.[284]

In other words, with very limited exceptions, Middle Eastern nations remain structurally dependent on the U.S. security umbrella. Even in cases where they are not (such as that of Israel), American cooperation – or at least acquiescence – is required for sustained regional action.

Targeting the Fault Lines

The third lesson has to do with adaptation. As the United States adapts to a world of great power rivalry, it will need to tailor its strategies to the unique political, cultural, and military contexts of each of today's potential adversaries. When it comes to nations like China, Russia, and Iran, deterrence relies on shaping the internal political calculations of adversaries. This is so for a simple reason. Authoritarian powers are not monoliths; they are brittle systems with real vulnerabilities. Recognizing and leveraging those shortcomings can amplify America's own freedom of action, and limit that of its adversaries.

---

283 See, for instance, "Bahrain's Armed Forces: Still Exclusive, Growingly Professional," Italian Institute for International Political Studies, July 9, 2024, https://www.ispionline.it/en/publication/bahrains-armed-forces-still-exclusive-growingly-professional-179508.

284 See, for instance, Dina Esfandiary, "How a Single Strike Rattled the Gulf's Illusion of Stability," *TIME*, July 1, 2025, https://time.com/7299042/strike-rattled-gulfs-illusion-of-stability/.

China

China's strategic posture is shaped by a blend of economic ambition, militaristic nationalism and centralized authoritarian control. Its recent behavior – from pressuring Taiwan to militarizing the South China Sea – suggests a regime deeply committed to securing expanded territorial claims and projecting power. Yet China is not monolithic. Minority populations in Tibet, Xinjiang, and Inner Mongolia, along with separatist sentiment in Hong Kong and latent resentment among ethnic minorities, represent significant points of potential pressure. So, too, do internal stressors like demographic decline, youth unemployment, and concerns over corruption – all of which threaten to erode the Chinese Communist Party's image of competence.

Another potential point of leverage is Chinese economic underperformance. After years of robust growth, the PRC's economy is now sputtering. The country's economic slowdown, driven by factors such as a property sector crisis and slowing consumer demand, has the potential to turn into a protracted recession, bringing with it growing domestic pressures and mounting popular discontent.[285]

U.S. strategy must factor in these internal dynamics. Informational campaigns that highlight the cost of military misadventures, the fragility of domestic consensus, or the real risk of defeat in Taiwan have the potential to give Chinese leaders pause. Likewise, bolstering third-party actors (such as Taiwan or Vietnam) via military and economic assistance can raise the cost to China of its coercive behavior, and help to deter more of it.

Russia

Moscow's recent military aggression (from Georgia to Crimea to Ukraine) has been fueled by a blend of imperial nostalgia, regional insecurity, and internal fragility. Putin's regime has succeeded in sustaining popular support in part by manufacturing external threats and claiming victories abroad.

---

285 See, for instance, Chris Lee, "China is on course for a prolonged recession," Australia Strategic Policy Institute *ASPI Strategist*, March 4, 2025, https://www.aspistrategist.org.au/china-is-on-course-for-a-prolonged-recession/#:~:text=Since%20local%20government%20debt%20is,demand%20would%20worsen%20economic%20imbalances..

However, Russia too is not as cohesive as it appears. The Russian Federation is a patchwork of ethnic regions, some of which crave independence and many of which contribute more in resources than they receive. These "donor oblasts" are increasingly restive, especially as the economic burdens associated with prolonged conflict continue to rise.[286]

In this context, the credibility of U.S. deterrence depends on exposing the costs of Russia's militarism. Publicizing the social costs of casualties, the decline in military readiness, and the economic degradation in donor regions can help drive wedges within the Russian state. Equally important is undermining the myth of Western weakness: NATO's cohesion, Ukraine's resilience, and Western industrial mobilization should be showcased as a way of dissuading further Russian adventurism.

Iran

Today's Iran combines a revolutionary foreign policy with deep domestic fragility. The regime's willingness to use proxies and asymmetric warfare is rooted in its belief that it can externalize internal discontent by positioning itself as the champion of both activist political Islam and resistance to Western hegemony. Yet inside Iran, pressures are mounting. The economy is battered by Western sanctions, corruption is endemic, and large portions of the population (especially ethnic minorities like Iran's Kurds, Baloch, and Arabs) feel alienated from the Persian-dominated state. Women, youth, and secular segments of society have also become increasingly, and openly, critical of the regime.

Here, America's response should be multidimensional. The United States must combine credible military threats, especially to Iran's proxy infrastructure, with information operations that amplify voices of dissent within Iranian society. Exposing elite corruption, highlighting regime hypocrisy, and supporting regional minorities can increase the costs associated with aggression to the Iranian regime. However, care must be taken

---

286   See, for instance, Evgeny Gontmakher, "Russia's uneven economic development," *GIS Reports*, September 16, 2021, https://www.gisreportsonline.com/r/russia-economic-development/.

to avoid provoking the Islamic Republic into fomenting an external war as a survival mechanism.

Rebuilding Capability Required

In order to accomplish these tasks, the United States will need to look inward and refocus on its domestic capabilities. As the National Defense Strategy Commission has counseled, it is no longer feasible for deterrence to be the purview of the Pentagon alone. Rather, it posits, a whole-of-nation approach that mobilizes the Executive Branch, private industry, and civil society is needed if the United States hopes to preserve its deterrence potential in today's new, adverse geopolitical environment.[287]

The criticism is apt. At present, the U.S. remains woefully unprepared for competing with – or effectively deterring – the new imperial impulses of China, Russia and Iran. The frailty begins with the current, suboptimal state of the U.S. defense-industrial base. As Larry Wortzel of the American Foreign Policy Council notes in a recent comparative study of the U.S. and Chinese defense industries, the American production base has shrunk precipitously – from 51 firms in 1993 to just five major companies today – while the United States is now increasingly dependent on distant nations (such as South Korea) for critical capabilities, risking a severing of supply lines in the event of conflict.[288]

Nor is there anything resembling a national mobilization of this sector on the horizon. Although more and more U.S. policymakers are aware of the centrality of U.S. defense production to both alliance credibility and America's own force projection capabilities, there is as yet no meaningful movement toward a recapitalization of this sector – or even of a legislative push to enable one. (A notable exception to this general malaise is the space sector and emerging space economy, where for the moment the United States still maintains significant "first mover" advantage. Nevertheless, here

287 *Report of the Commission on the National Defense Strategy* (Santa Monica: RAND, July 2024), https://www.armed-services.senate.gov/imo/media/doc/nds_commission_final_report.pdf.
288 Larry Wortzel, "Deterrence and the Industrial Base: the United States and China," AFPC *Special Report*, forthcoming Fall 2025.

too America's edge is eroding, as disjointed policy and the lack of a broad vision of space development risk ceding the advantage to the PRC, which has developed one.)[289]

The aggregate result is stark. As the National Defense Commission concludes, U.S. defense industrial production is alarmingly insufficient, incapable of generating the munitions, systems, and technologies needed to sustain prolonged conflict, let alone surge for great power war.[290]

This represents a critical deficiency. If America hopes to truly compete with China across the multiple domains that are now encompassed by "great power competition," it will need a truly national effort. This priority becomes even more urgent when America's strategic competition expands to include not only China but Russia and Iran as well.

The shortfall extends beyond defense industry. America's ability to reassure allies, strengthen partnerships, and influence foreign publics are atrophying as well. Worse, this appears to be happening by design. Since taking office in January 2025, the Trump administration has set about dismantling a significant portion of the U.S. federal bureaucracy. Some of these cuts are indeed warranted, a justified response to a federal government that has steadily grown in size and a foreign policy bureaucracy that in recent years has been plagued by both "mission creep" and inefficiency. But the wholesale elimination of agencies and functions – rather than their optimization and reform – has risked eliminating critical capabilities the country needs in order to truly compete internationally. So dramatic have these moves been that they have been equated to a "war on soft power."[291]

This is particularly visible in the information domain, where drastic cuts have caused American outreach to constrict precipitously. The United States Agency for Global Media (USAGM), the federal entity responsible for overseeing American international broadcasting, has been targeted for closure by the Administration, with its constituent parts either eliminated

---

289   See generally Richard M. Harrison and Peter Garretson, *The Next Space Race: A Blueprint for American Primacy* (Praeger Security International, 2023).

290   Ibid.

291   Keith Mines, "The War on Soft Power," *Jerusalem Strategic Tribune*, September 2025, https://jstribune.com/mines-the-war-on-soft-power/.

outright or repackaged in minimal form. Thus, the Administration's current plans call for a pared-down Voice of America to be folded into the U.S. Department of State, where it will exist and operate in truncated form. In the meantime, its Eurasia and Mandarin divisions, as well as its Persian Service, have shrunk dramatically, while its broadcasting to Africa and Latin America have ceased altogether. The broadcasting "grantees" – Radio Free Europe/Radio Liberty, the Middle East Broadcasting Networks, Radio Free Asia, and the Open Technology Fund – are likewise now struggling to survive. Since March 2025, each has taken the Administration to court to compel it to provide them with Congressionally appropriated funds. While those lawsuits have so far been successful, future U.S. government investments are not. As a result, the continued operation of these entities is very much an open question.[292]

As a result, the future of U.S. messaging – including outreach to Chinese, Russian and Iranian audiences, as well as global constituencies that Beijing, Moscow and Tehran are now attempting to woo to their side – is now deeply uncertain. The mismatch is all the more glaring when compared to the concerted investments that each of America's principal adversaries are making today in the informational domain. China under Xi has been estimated to spend $10 billion a year (or more) on external propaganda and influence operations.[293] Vladimir Putin's Russia, though resource-constrained as a result of the ongoing Ukraine war, is nonetheless investing heavily in propaganda; the country's 2025 budget is said to include 137 billion rubles (more than $1.4 billion) for television channels, media, and internet projects – a 13 percent increase over prior years.[294] And recent official allocations indicate that the Iranian regime now spends at least $600 million per year on such informational efforts,[295] with total annual spending

292   The authors have firsthand knowledge of these dynamics. One of them, Ilan Berman, was the head of the landing team for USAGM during the Trump 47 Transition, and now serves on the Boards of Directors of both Radio Free Europe/Radio Liberty and the Middle East Broadcasting Networks.

293   Ichihira Maiko, "China's Expanding Influence Operations: Online Propagandists Play the Long Game," *Nippon*, February 16, 2024, https://www.nippon.com/en/in-depth/d00971/.

294   "Where the Kremlin gets money to boost propaganda funding," Center for Countering Disinformation, October 7, 2024, https://cpd.gov.ua/en/results/where-the-kremlin-gets-money-to-boost-propaganda-funding/.

295   "Iran's Propaganda Budget Allocated with No Checks and Balances," *Iran International*, May 15, 2024, https://www.iranintl.com/en/202405139799.

(on both official and non-official initiatives in this domain) likely exceeding $1 billion.

America's ability to track and respond to Chinese, Russian and Iranian disinformation has likewise been hard hit. The State Department's recent reform and reorganization eliminated outright the Department's counter-disinformation bureau, known as the Global Engagement Center. While the GEC had previously come in for well-deserved criticism for its inefficiency and inherent bias,[296] its closure has had the effect of terminating U.S. support for foreign counter-disinformation efforts, thereby leaving a number of European allies more vulnerable to Russian disinformation.[297] Simultaneously, restructuring of the U.S. intelligence community by new Director of National Intelligence Tulsi Gabbard has led to a constriction in the scope and function of the Foreign Malign Influence Center, which "collects and analyzes data on foreign influence operations seeking to undermine U.S. democracy."[298] As a result, the United States is now significantly less capable of responding to – or even identifying – efforts by the PRC, the Russian Federation and the Islamic Republic to influence foreign publics against the West, and to destabilize democratic institutions within it.

Thus, the United States today appears to have prioritized "hard" power in its conduct of foreign affairs.[299] Notably, however, such an approach falls significantly short of the imperative of "integrated deterrence" called for by the National Defense Commission. It also makes the related imperatives of reassuring vulnerable allies, consolidating partnerships, and exploiting the fault lines among its adversaries that much harder to accomplish.

---

296   See, for instance, House Committee on Foreign Affairs, "McCaul, Mast, Issa send letter expressing concerns with GEC reauthorization," July 8, 2024, https://foreignaffairs.house.gov/news/press-releases/mccaul-mast-issa-send-letter-expressing-concerns-with-gec-reauthorization.

297   Ibid. See also Ilan Berman, *Countering Moscow's Message: Russian Disinformation and the Western Response* (AFPC Press, 2023).

298   Maggie Miller and Dana Nickel, "Gabbard to cut ODNI staff by nearly 50 percent," *Politico*, August 20, 2025, https://www.politico.com/news/2025/08/20/gabbard-odni-cuts-00517232.

299   Keith Mines, "The War on Soft Power," *Jerusalem Strategic Tribune*, September 2025, https://jstribune.com/mines-the-war-on-soft-power/.

Exploring The Limits of the New Axis

On June 13, 2025, the government of Israeli Prime Minister Benjamin Netanyahu launched what has come to be known as the "Twelve Day War." Over the span of a week, Israel's military carried out extensive strikes on Iran's complex, distributed nuclear program. It eliminated top officials in the country's military hierarchy and chain of command. And it succeeded in killing scores of senior Iranian nuclear scientists. Toward the end of this offensive, Israel's efforts were augmented by the United States, which used superior American ordinance to amplify the damage done to Iran's national nuclear project.

The cumulative effect was dramatic. Estimates of the resulting impact of the attacks on Iran's nuclear progress have varied widely, with the Trump administration claiming that Iran's atomic effort had been comprehensively destroyed as a result. Critics and detractors, meanwhile, have contended that the Israeli-American effort had resulted only in temporary, fleeting damage to the Iranian nuclear program. The truth likely lies in the middle; while the Iranian desire for nuclear status has not been fundamentally derailed, informed calculations suggest that the Israeli-American campaign succeeded in "significantly damaging" Iran's nuclear and ballistic missile program.[300]

The decision taken by the Trump administration was far from uncontroversial, however. Ahead of the conflict, many within President Trump's own party had warned of dire consequences of any such conflict. Personalities like Tucker Carlson and Candace Owens issued dire predictions about the consequences of action, warning that an Israeli campaign against Iran's nuclear program (and U.S. assistance to it) would inevitably lead to a regional war – or worse.[301]

Nothing of the sort happened, however. To be sure, both Chinese and Russian officials took pains to express solidarity with Iran.[302] They also

---

300 Emanuel Fabian and agencies, "IDF assesses Iran's nuclear program set back years, but 'too early' to know for sure," *The Times of Israel*, June 25, 2025, https://www.timesofisrael.com/idf-assesses-irans-nuclear-program-set-back-years-but-too-early-to-know-for-sure/.

301 Eli Lake, "They predicted World War III. They were Wrong," *The Free Press*, June 24, 2025, https://www.thefp.com/p/they-predicted-world-war-iii-they.

302 "Putin and Xi condemn Israel over its Iran strikes in phone call, Kremlin says," Reuters, June 19, 2025, https://www.reuters.com/world/china/russias-putin-chinas-xi-condemn-israel-over-its-iran-strikes-phone-call-kremlin-2025-06-19/.

issued statements roundly condemning the Israeli and American offensive. What they did not do, however, was provide the Islamic Republic with concrete support – in the form of weapons, defensive equipment, or technology – that could have been used to blunt the effectiveness of Israel's attack, or to raise the stakes for Jerusalem and Washington in their targeting of the Iranian regime's nuclear effort.

For the Islamic Republic, this passivity unquestionably has been deeply concerning. The Iranian regime has banked heavily in recent years on its alliances with both Moscow and Beijing to assist it in surviving amid deeply adverse geopolitical circumstances. As a consequence, the Iranian regime is now actively working to bolster those strategic partnerships further. In the aftermath of the "Twelve Day War," Iranian officials have sought to expand military contacts with the Kremlin in an effort to add concrete substance to the 20-year Comprehensive Strategic Partnership Treaty hammered out between the two nations earlier in 2025.[303] With China, too, Tehran has likewise sought tenser ties. In the immediate aftermath of the conflict in late June, Iranian Defense Minister Aziz Nasirzadeh traveled to Beijing in order to procure new high-end military equipment, including fighter jets and advanced radars.[304] Subsequently, at the July meeting of the Shanghai Cooperation Organization in Tianjin, China, Iran attempted to secure commitments from the PRC and other bloc members for stepped up strategic coordination.[305]

But if Iranian officials are now questioning the durability of their government's partnerships with Moscow and Beijing, national security experts in Washington need to be asking a different set of questions. As the foregoing pages have amply demonstrated, the growing "axis of upheaval" that has successfully been forged in recent years between Beijing, Moscow

303 Nigar Bayramii, "Iran, Russia Defense Ministers Discuss Expanding Military Cooperation," *Caspian News*, July 24, 2025, https://caspiannews.com/news-detail/iran-russia-defense-ministers-discuss-expanding-military-cooperation-2025-7-24-0/.

304 "Iran's Defense Minister Visits China in First Trip Since War," *Bloomberg*, June 25, 2025, https://www.bloomberg.com/news/articles/2025-06-25/iran-s-defense-minister-visits-china-in-his-first-trip-since-war.

305 See, for instance, Amira El-Fekki, "Iran Seeks Backing from China and Russia After U.S. Airstrikes," *Newsweek*, July 15, 2025, https://www.newsweek.com/iran-seeks-backing-china-russia-after-us-airstrikes-2099125.

and Tehran represents a cardinal strategic dilemma for the United States. It challenges American primacy, and U.S. interests, across multiple domains and in multiple world regions, from information to economy, and from Africa to Asia.

Yet, the recent conflict in the Middle East has amply demonstrated that this alignment is not absolute. "The Russia-Iran and PRC-Iran relationships, although certainly improved in recent years, have never been full-fledged alliances," a recent analysis by CNA, a Washington defense think tank, has noted. "Their strategic partnerships are limited and based on mutual interest and alignment."[306]

Identifying those trends, and their limits, is vital for American foreign policy. The new anti-Western axis that has emerged between the Chinese Communist Party, the Kremlin, and Iran's ayatollahs poses a threat not only to the United States and American interests, but to the Western order writ large. Beijing, Moscow and Tehran have unequivocally demonstrated that they harbor a shared desire to alter the rules of the road of the international system in their favor – and to the great detriment of the United States and its allies. Preventing them from doing so represents a core American national security interest, and a predicate for the prosperity that has typified the U.S.-led global order throughout the 20th Century.

As such, the fissures, limitations and contradictions of this tripartite partnership need to become the subject of serious study by American policymakers. Only by identifying – and then exploiting – the limits of the contemporary alliance among China, Russia and Iran can the United States successfully thwart the ambitions of today's new imperialists.

---

306 Elizabeth Wishnick and Julian G. Waller, "Russia And China Respond—Or Don't—To The 12-Day War In Iran," *CNA in-depth*, July 8, 2025, https://www.cna.org/our-media/indepth/2025/07/russia-and-china-respond-to-the-12-day-war-in-iran.

About the Authors

Herman Pirchner, Jr. became the founding President of the American Foreign Policy Council in 1982. Under his leadership, AFPC has emerged as a leading voice in the Beltway foreign policy debate and as a critical resource for U.S. lawmakers and officials in the Executive Branch on issues relating to national security and foreign affairs. During the 2012 Presidential campaign, Mr. Pichner directed the national security team advising former House Speaker Newt Gingrich. Earlier in his career, he served in the U.S. Senate as Director of Legislation for Sen. Roger Jepsen (R-IA), as well as Legislative Assistant to Senator Chuck Grassley (R-IA). Among his many publications are the prescient *Reviving Greater Russia: The Future of Russia's Borders with Belarus, Georgia, Kazakhstan, Moldova, and Ukraine* (University Press of America, 2005) and *Post Putin: Succession, Stability, and Russia's Future* (Rowman and Littlefield, May 2019).

Ilan Berman is the Senior Vice President of the American Foreign Policy Council. An expert on regional security in the Middle East, Central Asia, and the Russian Federation, he has consulted for the U.S. Central Intelligence Agency as well as the U.S. Departments of State and Defense, and has been called one of America's "leading experts on the Middle East and Iran" by CNN. He is the editor of six books, and the author of six others, including *Iran's Deadly Ambition: The Islamic Republic's Quest for Global Power* (Encounter Books, 2015) and, most recently, *Challenging Moscow's Message: Russian Disinformation and the Western Response* (AFPC Press,

2023). Mr. Berman is a member of the Associated Faculty at Missouri State University's Department of Defense and Strategic Studies, as well as an adjunct professor at the Institute of World Politics. He is a member of the Board of Directors of both *Radio Free Europe/Radio Liberty* and the Middle East Broadcasting Networks.

www.ingramcontent.com/pod-product-compliance
Lightning Source LLC
Chambersburg PA
CBHW032354280326
41935CB00008B/573